PRAISE
OUTNUMBER

"*Outnumbered 20 to 1* is a timeless pi ‿ ...story. Many military books are written by researchers who read between the lines to capture the feeling and dialogue, the sights, sounds, and smells of men in combat. However, not so with Colonel Bill Collier (Ret.). He was right in the middle of one of the most historic battles of the Vietnam War. Leadership cannot be taught; it is organic and part of your DNA. Major Collier led from the front and inspired his troops during this bloody 54-hour intense battle. This book is a story of hope, valor, and determination, and you'll be glad you picked it up."

—**John Ligator**,
U.S. Marine, Recipient of Three Purple Hearts and
the Bronze Star with a V for Valor, Retired FBI Agent
(8 years deep cover); Author of *The Dirty Boys*

"As I read through the story of the battle at Mo Duc found in these pages, I kept finding myself comparing Major Collier to Davy Crockett at the Alamo. He accomplished a Herculean defense of a seemingly impossible situation and came out victorious. That speaks great volumes about him as a person and his leadership abilities under fire. The highest compliment I can give Bill is that he is a leader of men I would follow into combat at any place and at any time."

—**Joseph A. Personett**,
Recipient of the Air Force Cross;
OV-10 Bronco Pilot during the Battle for Mo Duc;
30-year Commercial Airline Pilot (Ret.);
Department of Defense USAF Instructor Pilot

"When I started reading *Outnumbered 20 to 1*, I was shocked that I had never heard of this historic battle before. Being a Marine Vietnam veteran, I have watched hundreds of hours of video documentation and read many books about the war, but nothing more compelling than this battle. I couldn't believe this story wasn't part of our American history in Vietnam. The reader will find Army Colonel Bill Collier in the middle of one of the most historic battles of the Vietnam War. With the odds overwhelming, Major Collier led the South Vietnamese Army troops and civilians to victory only after days and nights of furious battles. This is a must-read for all military historians and veterans."

—**Danny Lane**,
Vietnam Veteran 1968-1969,
Author of *Some Gave it All* and *Code of Steel*

"Colonel Bill Collier's story is an amazing testament to the courage and enduring faith of so many who fought in Vietnam. As a fellow combat veteran (Afghanistan), I found Bill's account of facing such overwhelming and seemingly insurmountable odds uniquely inspiring. He and his men kept faith in God and each other to survive a ferocious battle."

—**William "Bill" V. Connor**,
Retired Army Colonel and Attorney

"A searing tale of high-intensity combat in Vietnam in which one man was thrust into assuming the mantle of battlefield command, which so many of the great captains of military history have assumed whenever there was a scarcity of and a necessity for the same. Colonel Bill Collier's story will serve as a timeless model of American combat leadership in a life-and-death struggle against all odds."

—**Maj. Gen. James E. Livingston**,
USMC (Ret.), Recipient of the Medal of Honor

OUTNUMBERED
20 TO 1

A VIETNAM WAR BIOGRAPHY

COL. WILLIAM COLLIER JR.

MADE FOR
SUCCESS

Made for Success Publishing
P.O. Box 1775 Issaquah, WA 98027
www.MadeForSuccessPublishing.com

Distributed by Made for Success Publishing

First Printing

Library of Congress Cataloging-in-Publication data

Collier, Col. William Jr.
     Outnumbered 20 to 1: A Vietnam War Biography
        p. cm.

LCCN: 2022917719
ISBN: 978-1-64146-759-9 *(Paperback)*
ISBN: 978-1-64146-760-5 *(ebook)*

Printed in the United States of America

For further information contact Made for Success Publishing
+14255266480 or email service@madeforsuccess.net

CONTENTS

ACKNOWLEDGMENTS

WRITING THIS BOOK was never a serious desire or intention of mine. Over the years since serving in Vietnam, I have learned that the vast majority of combat veterans from World War II up to and including Afghanistan have chosen to keep their experiences and memories mostly to themselves. This also was my sincere intention. However, certain events, organizations, and individuals throughout these many years eventually succeeded in altering my intentions.

My wife of 54 years, Patricia Shaull Collier, passed in December 2015. She knew more of my Vietnam stories than anyone else. Even so, she knew precious few of the stories and very little of how I felt about those experiences. To her credit, and thankfully so, she lovingly encouraged and prodded me throughout many years to record my Vietnam experiences. She was quite consistent in her prodding and suggestions and even bought me a tape recorder on two separate occasions, albeit to no avail. I am eternally grateful for my wife and her support. Her words of encouragement still resonate with me today as my principal motivator.

My daughter, Tricia Collier Richardson, always stated her desire for a written account of my wartime service as well. She has been a loud advocate for this book to be written. After the passing of my wife, Tricia relentlessly doubled down on her belief that it was time to write this book. She was an exceptionally strong encourager, especially during recent years. Thank you, Tricia. I heard you. I have appreciated your encouragement, and I love you for it.

My son-in-law, Alan L. Richardson, also agreed with my daughter's frequent attempts to initiate the stories relayed in this book. He was my constant go-to person for computer-related problems and other important sundry recommendations. Thank you, Alan.

One of my granddaughters, Samantha Erin Collier, very frequently mentioned that I needed to record my stories. Thank you, Samantha, for your encouragement and interest in my military service.

Longtime close personal friends since 1964, Lieutenant Colonel (Ret.), U.S. Army, Donald L. Ekstrom, and his wife Donna have also frequently insisted that I write this book. Don served with the 1st Cavalry Division (Airmobile) in 1965 and as a district advisor in the Mekong Delta in 1966. Don received two Purple Hearts, and he understood the need to describe the battle for Mo Duc. Thank you, Don and Donna.

I am very fortunate that several friends substantially helped me during the writing of this book. Each one possessed specific levels of knowledge and expertise that proved to be invaluable in terms of storyline content, editing, and overall preparation.

I jointly co-founded a combat veterans support organization in 2011 in Columbia, SC, with two members of my church, Colonel (Ret.) Steven B. Vitali, U.S. Marine Corps, a decorated combat commander of the wars in both Iraq and Afghanistan, and the Reverend W. Robert Farmer, a Vietnam combat veteran.

Col. Vitali soon learned more details of my Vietnam experiences than I had intended for anyone to know. As a personal friend and a prolific writer himself, Steve constantly pushed me to write this book. During this past year, he provided me with immeasurable assistance in its preparation, especially with events and details pertaining to the battle in and around Mo Duc. I also asked him to write the foreword to this book, which he graciously did. I am grateful for his willing guidance, editorial assistance, and friendship. Thank you, Steve.

I served with the 7th Battalion, 13th Artillery, during my first Vietnam tour. After returning to the United States from Vietnam, only a very few of the battalion's soldiers kept in contact with one another. In 2009, a former cannoneer in Battery C had a strong desire to reconnect with his wartime buddies. This young cannoneer, Robert R. Adams, later became a successful financial advisor. He spent a lot of time, effort, and money researching the battalion's wartime records and locating wartime members of the battalion. Robert laid the groundwork for our reunions and became our Association leader. In 2010, this battalion initiated the first of its now-annual reunions. These reunions have been life-changing events for many of the battalion's soldiers, including me. The reunions were another source of motivation for me to write this book. Thank you, Robert.

Several years later, one of the three forward observers, 1st Lieutenant Terry R. Lane, whom I served with as battery commander in 1967, attended the annual battalion reunion. Terry had trained with us at Ft. Irwin, CA, and had crossed the Pacific Ocean on the merchant marine ship transporting our battalion's equipment from California to Vietnam.

We served together our entire year in Vietnam. Terry was instrumental in helping me write this story, as he too had lived part of it. His advice and recall were incredibly valuable and helped with the accuracy of the events pertaining to my first tour. Thank you, Terry. Your assistance and recommendations were both very much appreciated.

A third member of my church and both an editor and journalist by profession, Colonel (Ret.) W. Thomas Smith, Jr., S.C. Military Dept., provided assistance to our combat veterans group from time to time. Tom is a former U.S. Marine infantry leader who, as an embedded journalist, spent time overseas in four wars, including twice in Iraq. He is a well-known published writer on many levels (and a *New York Times* bestselling editor) who offered to assist with the preparation of this book.

Subsequently, Tom conducted a detailed editing of this manuscript and offered very perceptive corrections, comments, and suggestions, but always kept the work in my voice. Having Tom's expertise in the preparation of this book was a true blessing. His was not an easy chore, for which I will be eternally grateful. I also asked him to write the afterword to this book, which he did. For your expertise, time, and friendship, thank you very much, Tom.

I also want to recognize and thank the friends and fellow soldiers who participated in our previously mentioned combat veterans support group, as well as the unnamed friends and family members who have encouraged and supported me in this effort. Thank you, all.

Lastly, I want to recognize the unselfish and successful participation of the many unsung and unnamed heroes during the battle for Mo Duc. They are the joint service participants who flew U.S. Army helicopters, U.S. Air Force OV-10 Broncos flown by forward air controllers, carrier-based U.S. Navy A-7 Corsairs, either USAF or U.S. Marine Corps aviators who launched F-4 Phantom jets from Ubon, Thailand, and several U.S. Navy ships positioned in the South China Sea, especially the USS Hanson and her great crew. I witnessed firsthand the actions of so many Americans willing to put themselves in grave danger necessary to save other Americans. To these wonderful American military personnel, I sincerely thank you.

—*WPC*

FOREWORD

THE BATTLE FOR MO DUC is an extraordinary and heartfelt chapter from the Vietnam War that has been largely forgotten, perhaps even hidden, from our illustrious military history and legacy—that is, until now.

As the last significant battle in the war, Mo Duc speaks to the greater American military tradition and significantly showcases the valiant efforts of those freedom-desiring, albeit ill-fated South Vietnamese soldiers who made their last stand, winning the battle, though not the war.

Standing on the command precipice was then Major (today retired Colonel) Bill Collier, whose defiant stance against overwhelming odds served as the juggernaut and protagonist against the strategic and political ambitions of the North Vietnamese leadership.

Bill was and will forever be All-Army and an All-American. Today, in 2022, Bill is an active 80-plus-year-old retired combat leader; then, he was a tall, lanky American Army artillery officer who spoke with a tidewater Southern drawl and exhibited an easy-going demeanor on the battlefield, which belied his true persona as a ferocious warrior and sturdy combat commander.

At the start of the Mo Duc siege, Collier quickly assumed command of the beleaguered South Vietnamese garrison, assuming overall command due to the dearth of leadership and unhesitatingly faced off against a fiercely determined North Vietnamese Army (NVA) division at least 20 times greater in size.

For the next 54 hours, heralded exploits, unabated terror, epic ferocity, extreme sacrifices, unyielding compassion, and innate leadership permeated the beleaguered outpost as all hell broke loose from the air, the sea, and upon the very ground being defended. The continuous close combat and earth-shattering fireworks on and around the battlefield resulted in scores killed and badly wounded on both sides.

The cries of the wounded, the dying, and even the unscathed and afraid filled the air. And all were afraid: Bill himself confesses his own personal fear, though fear never overcame the sense of duty, compassion, and a fighting spirit so required in a combat leader.

Mo Duc ended in a magnificent victory, though, as Bill explains, not without God's intervention at critical periods in the fighting. According to Bill, were it not for the omnipotent presence of the Almighty, he and his small force surely would have been annihilated. And the enemy was taking no prisoners.

To save Bill and his men from total destruction, all elements of our sister services were drawn into the fight, and they forged a beautifully orchestrated offshore and overhead concert of supporting fires, with young Major Bill Collier as its deadly conductor.

Mo Duc was a fight for survival in the depths of great despair, yet Bill never lost his steely nerve nor his love for—and trust in—God. Being willing to sacrifice himself rather than harm the adjacent Mo Duc village and its civilian population, in all likelihood, saved his life.

Bill and I became close friends. Following his retirement from the Army after more than three decades of distinguished service, we met at Northeast Presbyterian Church (NEPC) in Columbia, SC, and soon thereafter became members of the NEPC Combat Veterans Support Group, supporting other veterans with their PTSD struggles. During one of our meetings, Bill provided a detailed account of the battle. At the end of the meeting, each veteran expressed unanimous disbelief that Bill had only received the Silver Star for his actions instead of the Medal of Honor (often unofficially referred to as the Congressional Medal of Honor), the nation's highest award for combat valor.

In the ensuing research as to why, we quickly learned that Bill would only receive the Silver Star as the Army had no American "eyewitnesses" at ground zero to corroborate his account of what happened during those harrowing 54 hours of hell on earth. The only other American on the ground with Bill during the siege was killed on the first afternoon.

The U.S. Army had largely withdrawn its forces from Vietnam prior to the Mo Duc battle in late 1972, leaving only advisory teams to continue training and mentoring the South Vietnamese forces. In 1972, there were ongoing political negotiations between the U.S. and its allies and Communist North Vietnamese negotiators to end the war, so Bill's decisive victory was tapped down in the press. In my opinion, the U.S. Army in Vietnam expedited a Silver Star award for Bill in order to put the Mo Duc saga behind them.

Unfortunately for Bill, the military's rush to put the battle (and, more broadly, the war) behind them was an injustice to an American hero and one of their (our) own. The Silver Star is the highest combat valor award allowed without physical eyewitnesses on the ground.

We quickly found two eyewitnesses of the Mo Duc siege, former U.S. Air Force captains—both forward air controllers—who were then flying an OV-10 attack-and-observation aircraft over Mo Duc. The men were in constant radio and, at times, visual contact with Bill on the ground.

Captain (today retired Colonel) Richard Poling and Captain Joseph Personett both confirmed that Bill's successful and heroic combat leadership, in the face of what would be impossible odds to any adept military mind, indeed warranted the Medal of Honor.

Poling and Personett were (and are) not just any eyewitnesses either: Both of these men are recipients of the nation's second-highest award, the Air Force Cross, for their actions in support of Bill's defense of Mo Duc. With the support of Col. (Ret.) Poling, Personett signed a request to officially upgrade Bill's Silver Star to the Medal of Honor.

Regardless of the award outcome, the undaunted bravery, determination, and heroic leadership of Bill in that desperate fight cannot be overstated. Bill believed—or, as he says, he "knew"—he was going to die, yet he remained calm and deliberate.

Without Bill's leadership, the garrison would have doubtlessly been annihilated.

Together, Poling and Personett write: "It was fantastic, truly indescribable! This one U.S. Army major and his small band of valiant men had just met an expertly trained and equipped force over 20 times their size and handed them an ignominious defeat. We later learned through intelligence sources that each NVA wore a sash which proclaimed their overwhelming victory and 'Liberation of Mo Duc.'"

It was indeed an "ignominious defeat" that was possible due to the clear-thinking competence and courage displayed by Bill at Mo Duc in mid-September 1972. Now, for the record, we have Bill's book, a highly readable account written with the same deft charm that those who know him best will quickly recognize, and all will enjoy.

Outnumbered 20 to 1 should be required reading for any developing military leader and combat commander. It is, frankly, an indispensable primer on combat leadership.

—*Colonel (Ret.) Steven B. Vitali, U.S. Marine Corps*
combat veteran of the Iraqi and Afghanistan Wars

INTRODUCTION

T HE BATTLE FOR MO DUC WAS ONE, if not *the* last, of the major battles of the Vietnam War… and it was a battle that hardly anyone had heard of. A vastly outnumbered group of various South Vietnamese military forces successfully defended their position for several days against elements of the North Vietnamese Army and the Viet Cong.

I was part of a small team of advisors on the ground inside the Mo Duc District headquarters compound that assisted in its defense. I believe that my previous training and experience, along with the help of God, are the reasons why what could have been the Vietnamese Alamo instead became a great victory.

Elements of all four traditional branches of the U.S. military— the Army, Navy, Marine Corps, and Air Force—contributed significantly to this victory, and this work is intended to recognize their contributions, skills, and heroism.

Events described in this book influenced my life going forward to a greater extent than I realized—until many years later. I have since talked with several others who participated in or were involved in some way or another with the battle, and I learned that it also remained part of their lives throughout the ensuing years.

Here is my attempt at re-telling the story, beginning with the start of my journey with the U.S. Army. I hope you gain as much in my re-telling as I gained in reconstructing my memories of this defining moment in my life, and in U.S. military history.

—Col. (Ret.) William P. "Bill" Collier, U.S. Army

CHAPTER ONE
REAL FIELD ARTILLERY TRAINING

E ARLY IN THE SPRING OF 1966, life was good for this young artillery captain stationed at Fort Sill, OK. Following graduation in 1960 from the University of Richmond (Virginia), including the Army Reserve Officers' Training Corps (ROTC) program, I entered active duty for the required two years. At that time, it had not crossed my mind that I would still be on active duty six years later. In fact, had such been suggested by anyone at that time, I would have been the first to veto the probability. To fulfill my advanced ROTC service obligation required attendance in the Field Artillery Officers Basic Course (FAOBC) and completion of two years of active duty as a Reserve Officer.

That was fair enough, as I did not have definitive career-oriented plans for my life in 1960.

After completing the FAOBC, my first assignment was with the Field Artillery Army Training Center (ATC), also located at Fort Sill. There were seven training battalions in the ATC. The first five battalions, numbered and identified sequentially, trained basic-training graduates to become artillery cannoneers. To the best of my recall, all cannoneer training was conducted on the 105 mm howitzer M101A1. The 7th Battalion trained recent basic training graduates to be either fire direction manual computers or artillery surveyors. These six battalions were known as advanced individual training (AIT) battalions.

The 6th Training Battalion, known as a basic unit training battalion, received graduates from the other AIT battalions, where they trained for six weeks to learn to function as a complete artillery firing battery. This training fulfilled the six-month active-duty training requirement for young men entering the service under the provisions of the Reserve Forces Act of 1955. Although I did not realize it at that time, I was extremely fortunate to be assigned to the 6th Training Battalion.

The military environment was a hugely different, strange, and sometimes hostile one for those like me who had no previous close family ties or experience with any of the military services. And I had to be one of the greenest individuals ever to receive a commission in the U.S. Army.

The officers in my first unit, B Battery (B-6), consisted of five commissioned officers. The battery commander (BC) was Capt. Thomas W.E. Smith, who served as an enlisted soldier in Germany during World War II and received a battlefield commission during the Korean conflict. The executive officer (XO), First Lieutenant James Moorehead, was an ROTC graduate and nearing the end of his two-year active-duty obligation. The three second lieutenants, Ken Halfacre, Fire Direction Officer (FDO); Bob Stewart, Recon and Survey Officer (RSO); and I, Forward Observer (FO), were assigned to the artillery battery within the previous two months. All lieutenants were ROTC grads except Lt. Halfacre, who was a recent Officer Candidate School graduate. All five officers were Reserve officers.

The battery's non-commissioned officer (NCO) Corps was populated with an array of intelligent, seasoned, and combat-experienced men who were absolutely amazing trainers. Several of them held battlefield commissions. However, after the war, they had to revert to their highest enlisted rank previously held, usually either because of a lack of a college education or a reduction in the military services after the war. First Sergeant Basil Simmons was one of them. For the first few months in the battery, I must admit that

I was scared of the NCOs. They were so knowledgeable and comfortable in the Army that whenever I encountered any one of them, I did not know whether to salute him, call him "sir," or run and hide from him. Of course, all three were inappropriate responses.

Among those wonderful NCOs was Sergeant First Class (SFC) Alonso E. Jordan. He was a WWII and Korean War veteran who not only had several Purple Hearts but was still carrying some shrapnel in his back and several tiny pieces in his cheek. His job was the chief of the firing battery (CFB). He was affectionately called "Smoke." No one called him by his name, rank, or job title. From the battery commander to the lowest-ranking enlisted man, he was addressed as either "Smoke" or "Hey, Smoke." He would not have it any other way.

The day that I drove into the battery parking area to report for duty in B Battery, 6th Training Battalion, in Ft. Sill, OK, in November 1960 set in motion experiences that would guide and change my life from then until this day. Nothing that followed that day was in my life's plans or wildest dreams. Until that day, this young, naïve, green lieutenant who grew up in Portsmouth, VA, in sight and smell of Scots Creek and the Elizabeth River, fully intended to return to his roots and spend much of his life playing in the creek and on the river.

SFC Alonso "Smoke" Jordan played a significant role in sidelining the plans I had for my life.

First Sgt. Simmons had assigned SFC Jordan to watch for my arrival. As I stepped out of my new 1961 black Volkswagen bug, SFC Jordan bellowed for me to follow him to the BC's office.

The walk from my car to the orderly room was a short distance. So much happened during that short walk. First, I was expecting a salute from SFC Jordan. He did not salute me. As I was conjuring up the courage to chew him out for not saluting me, the second incident occurred. SFC Jordan told me that I had been assigned to him and that he would make me a good artillery lieutenant if I kept my mouth shut and did what he told me.

Now, I need to say that, at this point, SFC Jordan was unable to adequately express himself unless he laced every sentence with an abundance of profanity. Although I am not a saint, I was not accustomed to so much profanity. He also held me by my left arm between my elbow and shoulder. I was thinking that nothing like this had ever been discussed in the training platform in college, ROTC summer camp at Fort Knox, or FAOBC. It just did not seem right. Before I could muster the appropriate words to rebuke SFC Jordan, we were at the orderly room door.

I was still trying to comprehend the fact that SFC Jordan had not saluted me, not to mention digest all he had said to me and how I should respond, when the First Sergeant (1stSgt) yelled, "Come in, lieutenant."

What the hell was going on? Things were happening faster than this Virginia boy could keep up with.

I entered the orderly room, and the BC yelled, "Come in, Collier." *Does everyone yell around here? Don't they know proper military procedure and courtesy?* I walked into the BC's office, and there sat an old man who looked like he should have been buried yesterday. Had he not been chain-smoking cigarettes, I might have called for the coroner.

I saluted and said, "Lt. Collier reporting for duty, sir."

"Aw crap, sit your ass down, Collier." He did not return my salute.

Maybe they don't salute in this training command, I thought. *OK, I will stop saluting, too.*

That turned out to be a mistake.

Within minutes, this old half-dead-looking captain had me eating out of his hand, so to speak. He seemed to know the state of shock and confusion I was in. Within a 15-minute discussion, he explained the mission of the battery and how the various positions and job skills were supposed to function in order to have a smooth-operating effective battery capable of accomplishing its mission in combat. He made me believe that being the forward observer

(FO) was the most important job in the battery. If I did not do my job correctly, then the entire battery would fail to accomplish its mission. More importantly, lives could be lost as a result.

I was anxious to get to my job and do it well. I wanted to make my new father figure (er, maybe I should say *grandfather* figure) proud of me. He read me like a book! As it turned out, he was a great commander and teacher. He was demanding but fair. And he made fun of his officers' mistakes but then left it at that, as long as we did not make the same mistake twice. I was comfortable working for and being around him.

The training cycle was six weeks. Weeks one and six were primarily dedicated to classroom instruction. All newly assigned lieutenants were required to take a two-week leadership and platform training instruction course before they could teach in the classroom.

Weeks two through five were field training weeks. The battery convoyed to the field each Tuesday morning and convoyed back to garrison each Thursday evening. Intense training occurred for 18 hours on each of those days. Mondays were classroom instruction and preparation for the movement to the field. Thursday evenings and Friday mornings were recovery operations, which really meant washing the guns and vehicles and accounting for all equipment. Saturday mornings were formal equipment, barracks, and personnel inspections by the battery commander and the 1stSgt.

Anyone coming up short in any area could look forward to spending the rest of Saturday correcting his shortcomings. And those personnel provided the 1stSgt his special duty personnel for his special projects on Sunday. Of course, this was before the Army eliminated Saturdays as a workday.

During field training, the two most junior lieutenants had to jointly perform the duties of safety officer on the guns. We wore helmet liners painted yellow. The proposed firing positions for the upcoming training week in the field were provided to us the preceding Friday. All safety data had to be prepared and approved by Battalion Operations Section by noon the next Monday. Lt. Stewart and I shared this duty with the FDO and, infrequently, the XO relieved us from time to time. Usually, I would FO on Tuesdays and Wednesdays and Lt. Stewart on Thursdays. I spent most of the time as the FO because I was the junior officer. Several months later, I realized how much I was looking forward to and enjoying the weekly field training events.

We trained on the Quanah Parker Range on the west range. It was difficult to lug our equipment up and down the mountain each day. It took about an hour to climb the mountain and select a different observation post (OP) each day. We were not allowed to use the same OP day after day.

Yeah... Right!

I soon learned that it was rare for someone to climb up to visit our OP. Maybe we occupied the same OPs more frequently than the BC was aware. If we made a mistake while observing artillery missions, it was readily apparent, and everyone knew. Even so, it was fun, to a certain extent, with a greater degree of autonomy than I had in the firing battery position.

Little did I realize the lasting impact SFC Jordan would have on my life that first morning I met him in the battery parking lot and was escorted by him to the commander's office. Who is this person called "Smoke"? Unfortunately, I did not learn much about Smoke's background, family, or his daily life outside the battery. I regret that very much. I failed to realize the enormous impact he had on my military career until many years after he had passed from this earthly life. I can now describe him somewhat and know his heart somewhat as well.

Whenever Smoke was observed walking through the battery area or in tactical field locations, you immediately knew who he was. Smoke stood about 5'9" or 5'10," and his somewhat unusual gait allowed his upper body to arrive at any destination one step before his lower body. His shoulders were not necessarily hunched over; it was simply the way he carried himself. Had he stood a bit more erect, he may have been an inch or two taller.

Smoke's face revealed a combination of youthful acne scars and the result of limited battle wounds. With deep-set eyes, he appeared profoundly serious most of the time. When unhappy, one would be wise to head for the hills... or, at the very least, get out of his sight for a while. However, Smoke's infrequent smile was warm and inviting. His heart and character were pure gold. His love of our nation, our Army, its soldiers, and the field artillery were unmistakably obvious. He epitomized the "soldier's soldier." I realized later in life how much I admired the man professionally for many reasons. He was always good to his word. He taught me to be a competent field artilleryman and officer.

During field training periods, I became an unofficial trainee under Smoke. After the battery conducted either a deliberate or hasty position occupation, the XO and CFB would "lay the six gun-tubes for common direction." This meant that all howitzer tubes were parallel to each other and pointed in the same direction of the azimuth of fire. That was the first and most important function to perform immediately after a position occupation, concurrent with a skeleton perimeter sweep. Other ongoing position functions included the selection of locations for the executive officer post, latrine, field mess, officers' tent, ingress and egress, switchboard, powder bag burn, and perimeter defense.

The battery can be laid for direction using several methods. Ft. Sill only allowed the use of an M2 aiming circle (AC) using an approved azimuth of fire or surveyed data already definitively identified. Smoke taught me to verify the lay of the battery using whichever system the XO had not used to lay the battery. Use of the aiming circle required serious attention to many preparation steps. He would sabotage my AC without telling me and watch to see if I would re-check my data. A great way to teach and learn. At the same time, it was extremely frustrating and irritating, especially early in his training of me.

As I progressed in the techniques that he wanted me to know and do, Smoke added more requirements. He taught me to float the needle (orient the AC on magnetic north) and get comfortable using that method to shoot artillery. Next came the use of a magnetic compass and, again, shooting artillery. That took courage on my part, as it is the least accurate. We shot rounds using this method. I guess I am safe in saying, some 60 years later, that our approach was contrary to Ft. Sill's range regulations. Additional training included bore-sighting procedures and how to observe the gun line to see if a gun might not be laid correctly.

I commanded two firing batteries in my career, one in combat. Smoke's training lessons allowed me to be comfortable during live fire and confident deciding that all was OK or what appropriate corrective action to take when needed. *Thank you, Smoke.* He also showed me how to lay by sunspot and Polaris at night. I never was confident with those and would not shoot using these methods. *Sorry about that, Smoke.*

The importance of a strong defensive perimeter can best be told by using two examples from my experience in Vietnam several years after Smoke's valuable instruction. In Vietnam, I was Service Battery commander for three months and Alpha Battery commander for eight months in the 7th Battalion 13th Artillery supporting the 1st Air Cavalry's operations in Vietnam from 1966-1967. My soldiers knew I checked and insisted on a strong perimeter defense. We were probed several times without a subsequent attack.

It was an entirely different story during my second Vietnam tour, 1972-1973. The Army of the Republic of Vietnam (ARVN) infantry battalion my four-man team was advising opted to live in the field rather than in a seemingly safer area. Following the Battle for Mo Duc in September 1972, this ARVN battalion was sent in to reinforce local units and help repel elements of the North Vietnamese Army (NVA). (The Mo Duc battle will be discussed in more detail in subsequent chapters.)

The ARVN battalion commander and I quickly developed a good working relationship, primarily based on my previous actions during the Mo Duc siege and the fact that I spoke a little Vietnamese.

I expressed my concerns that his late evening and nightly perimeters might be easy for local Viet Cong (VC) or NVA to penetrate. I do not think he appreciated my comments. That evening, he invited me to inspect his perimeter with him. My comments were frank. His perimeter was weaker than it should have been. It then became routine for his men to see their commander and me walking the perimeter each evening, making spot adjustments.

This battalion relocated frequently. This was in early October 1972. One night in November 1972, around 2300 hours, we were attacked by a sizable NVA force. A few NVA soldiers penetrated our perimeter but more than 10 NVA soldiers died in the attempt. Their attempt ended in a horrific less-than-30-minute battle and was wholly unsuccessful. Although he never mentioned the effectiveness of his perimeter defense against the attempted penetration, his relationship with me and his increased attention to the daily perimeter were obvious.

Several days later, the battalion commander was late returning from higher headquarters. I had not gone with him (was not invited) on the chopper. As evening was beginning, the ARVN battalion XO told me that several of his NCOs wanted me, the "CoVan My Thieu Ta" (American Advisor Major), to walk the perimeter. What an honor!

Smoke's influence on me continued to be present. *Thank you again, Smoke. From the grave, you once again saved my life and the lives of numerous of my South Vietnamese warriors.*

Back to the 6th Training Battalion at Ft. Sill, I moved up to become the FDO after 10 months as an FO. In March 1962, the battalion commander reassigned me to Charlie Battery (C-6) as the XO, coinciding with my promotion to first lieutenant.

Charlie Battery had 155-mm howitzers. Its "bullets" were larger than the 33-pound 105-mm rounds of B Battery, weighing in at approximately 95 pounds each. Capt. Sweiven, an aviator, and 1stSgt. Emilio were the battery's senior leadership. Both were Korean War veterans and quite willing to let me control the daily operations.

SO THAT'S HOW THE ARMY WORKS!

On November 19, 1961, I married a beautiful young woman, Patricia Mae Shaull, who became my best friend, and the mother of our 3 children until God took her home in 2015 after 54 years of marriage.

While beginning to think about life after the Army as a civilian and married man, I learned that several lieutenants in ATC had opted to go "voluntary indefinite." This extended their active duty one additional year as a minimum and eliminated the requirement to attend several years of monthly reserve meetings as civilians.

My separation date was the end of September 1962, and we were expecting our first child in December 1962. I decided to let the Army pay for the birth of my son, allowing me another year to decide what and where my civilian life would be a year from that point, with no reserve meetings to factor into the equation. In truth, I was enjoying ATC, all of which sounded like the right course of action to take at that time. I signed on the dotted line, planning on separating from the Army in September 1963 instead of 1962.

Then the Cuban Missile Crisis occurred in October 1962, one month into my third active-duty Army year. One evening around 2100 hours, Capt. Sweiven summoned my wife and me to his home, where, upon arriving, we found his wife crying. He was leaving in the morning for Florida to participate in actions against Cuba. I was handed a few rings of keys and told to inventory all the property and assume command of C Battery.

Maybe I should have separated last month when I had the chance! I thought. *Well, OK, I* did *enjoy the unit.* I reasoned that being the BC would be a good experience. Two months later, I received orders assigning me to Korea in March 1963 for 13 months.

So *that's* how the Army works!

I departed for Korea in early March 1963, leaving behind a bride of 16 months and a son, William III, only 3 months old. I was not a particularly happy camper and seriously questioned some of my decision-making abilities. Upon arriving at Travis Air Force Base, some 50 miles north of San Francisco, CA, several lieutenants were pulled aside and told we were going to Korea on a troopship, the USNS Edwin D. Patrick. The ocean trip would count as part of our 13-month tour. We were given temporary duty (TDY) pay and one week in San Francisco to do anything we wanted during the day while reporting in each evening at 2300 hours. Uncle Sam was paying us to see the sights of San Francisco. What a sweet deal.

It was an uneventful, enjoyable 18-day voyage to Korea. We crossed the 180 Meridian, also known as the International Date Line (IDL), and we were subjected to an initiation "celebrating" the crossing.

We arrived at the famous Inchon Harbor and disembarked on March 22, 1963.

My assignment with the First Cavalry Division on the Demilitarized Zone (DMZ) as a battery XO and Division Artillery Assistant Communications Officer was somewhat scary and clearly sobering. There were too many "what ifs" and "when ifs" about the North Koreans attacking across the DMZ. It was pleasant duty, albeit somewhat confining with limited movement allowed only on the mostly unimproved dirt roads.

Early in the morning of November 22, 1963, the battery's sirens started blaring. We were placed on high alert and told to break out the ammunition. *Were we about to be attacked by the North Koreans?* My adrenaline was surging! *Why did I go voluntary indefinite? I could be a civilian somewhere in the U.S., safe and secure.* After several hours, we learned that President John F. Kennedy had been assassinated in Texas. We remained on full alert for 24 hours just in case the North Koreans wanted to do something foolish.

At times, it can get extremely cold in Korea. Someone in Division HQ with a weird sense of humor was very proficient at scheduling field training exercises during some of the coldest periods of winter. During one field training exercise, several lieutenants, myself included, were selected to be liaison officers to various South

Korean units of the First Capital Republic of Korea Division, better known as the Tiger Division.

Strict adherence to field training requirements was enforced. I spent the first day and night in the 1st Cavalry Division artillery tactical operations center. Shortly before dusk on the second exercise day, my driver and I were provided map coordinates of the Tiger Division unit we were going to co-locate with for the remainder of the exercise. That unit's location required the use of two different map sheets and was east of and outside of the 1st Cavalry Division's normal area of operations. Thankfully, the maps were in English.

I studied the maps and plotted a route to get us there in the shortest amount of time. Our Jeep could not have any canvas on it, the windshield had to be laid down on the motor's hood, and black-out driving conditions were to be observed at all times. Our Jeep was essentially an open-air convertible with no doors. We started our journey to the assigned Korean Army unit after dark, and it was *cold*... and getting colder with each passing minute. After several hours of shivering uncontrollably while reading a map through a red plastic filter placed over the military flashlight, I wasn't confident that I really knew where we were. However, my driver had complete confidence in me.

Why? Because he had no other choice.

Somewhere outside of the Division/American area, as we slowly drove about 10 miles per hour, we could hear tanks rumbling nearby. I told my driver to stop a bit off the road. If I could not see the tanks, then they couldn't see us. Within several minutes, the tanks rumbled past us. The heat from their rear engines was so very welcome. Maybe they were going to the unit we were trying to get to. I instructed my driver to drive behind the rear tank because it was warm there. So warm, in fact, that we unbuttoned several buttons on our parkas. We followed them for 30 or 40 minutes and into a Korean compound. They were totally surprised to see us in our Jeep. No one spoke English, and, of course, neither of us spoke Korean.

After a period of talking to each other and no one understanding anything, an English-speaking Korean captain appeared. *Now, what do I do?*

Graciously, the captain invited us to his hooch to get warm and enjoy a small meal. We accepted. At that point, the time was approaching 2300 hours. I showed him the coordinates of our destination, which he indicated was too far away to get to that night. So, we spent the night in a spartan-type building kept minimally warm. After a strange breakfast of noodles and some type of meat and hard bread, the captain outlined the road network we should take to continue on to the Korean unit. At that point, it dawned on me that no one had tried to contact me even though we were supposed to arrive last night—no one seemed to know where we were or even care. We could have mistakenly gone into North Korea, and no American would have known.

What was I supposed to have done in my role as a liaison officer to that Korean artillery headquarters? *Face being court-martialed? Or at the very least be subjected to a rigorous ass-chewing, which I deserved?*

My decision was to maintain radio silence, return to my First Cavalry Division artillery battery, and prepare to take whatever punishment my captain or his lieutenant colonel would impose on me. My driver was above blame. He was simply following my orders.

Upon arrival in our battery area, I helped wash and clean up the Jeep, trying to delay the inevitable as long as possible. To this day, no one has ever said a word about any of this to me. I genuinely believe they forgot all about me. Several months later, while performing duties as compound officer of the guard, my driver and I drank a toast to our good fortune and swore never to mention this event.

First Cavalry Division officers departing Korea for reassignment to the U.S. were required to fill out a "dream sheet" stating their assignment preferences. Mine was brief and to the point: "Send me anywhere you want as I intend to be released from active duty in a few months after returning to the U.S."

The division personnel staff sergeant major (SSM) asked me to come visit him, which I did. He recommended I redo my dream sheet to "request attendance at the Field Artillery Officers Advanced Course above all other considerations." That was all I was to write. His rationale was that attendance in the Advanced Course as a First Lieutenant was uncommon and would be a plus for me. Should I decide in the future to go into the Army Reserve or the National Guard, I would already be educationally qualified for promotion through major. The Advanced Course was only about five months long, and then I could be on my way to wherever I wanted. Great advice from the SSM. I was pleased that we had caring SSMs like him in the Army. I accepted his recommendation and, once again, signed on the dotted line.

Will I ever learn?

After 13 months in Korea, I was reassigned to Ft. Sill to attend the Field Artillery Officers Advanced Course. The Advanced Course was professionally beneficial and enjoyable. My wife and I made some lifelong friends, learned about the military's social life and customs, and saw another side of Army life we had heretofore never seen.

A month before graduation, I visited the personnel office to request *Release from Active Duty* (RFAD) Orders and travel to Portsmouth, VA. The personnel officer's response was incredulous.

While a student in the Advanced Course, I had been promoted to captain. He informed me that attendance at the Advanced Course incurred a year of active duty beginning upon completion of the course. He was incredulous that I did not know that, but I had no recollection of the SSM in Korea telling me that information.

Further, he had orders for me to be the battery commander of the 2nd Enlisted Student Battery in the school brigade. I had been selected in consideration of my extensive troop duty thus far in my career. *What?!* The enlisted student batteries are fraught with student personal problems. He said the board believed my background made me ideally suited for this assignment. In absolute shock, I stumbled out of his office.

Are they ever going to let me out of the Army? Surely, I am dreaming!

A year later, I realized that this Battery Command turned out to be a wonderful job and time in my life. I had a second child, a beautiful baby daughter named Tricia. My wife was enjoying military life as well.

Maybe I should stay in for another 14 years until retirement. Might even get assigned to Germany. People say Germany is a great assignment. Good plan. Life is good.

This plan was not to be.

* * *

Whoops! Just received orders for reassignment to Italy, departing in June 1966.

We were incredibly pleased, and my off-again, on-again decision to remain in the Army was made. Off to the innocuous personnel office again—this time, to request an application for a commission as a regular Army officer and remain in the Army as a career. How is that for a 180-degree change in direction? Once again, I signed on the dotted line.

And now you have it—the short version of how I came to serve on active duty for 30 years!

CHAPTER TWO
REACTIVATION OF THE 7TH BATTALION, 13TH ARTILLERY RED DRAGONS

L IFE CONTINUED TO BE GOOD, especially once I had decided to make the Army a career "on my terms." Four or five more months as a BC in the School Brigade and then off to Italy: That was the plan. But the Army had other plans. A new set of orders arrived dated April 14, 1966, that assigned me to the 7th Battalion 13th Artillery at Ft. Irwin, CA, with a reporting date of June 1, 1966.

The 7th Battalion, 13th Artillery was being reconstituted as a 105-mm howitzer battalion. The battalion would have a headquarters and headquarters battery, three howitzer firing batteries, and a service battery responsible for second-echelon maintenance functions and all battalion logistical support. June 1 was its re-activation date, which happened to coincide with my reporting date. I do not recall a re-activation ceremony.

Located in the Mojave Desert, Ft. Irwin had been known as the California Armor and Desert Training Center for many years before the name change from Camp Irwin to Fort Irwin in the early 1960s. The post was hot and dry, with a paucity of signage to guide incoming personnel to various locations.

A second 105-mm howitzer battalion (7th Battalion 9th Artillery) and two Army signal companies (5th Company 86th Signal and 5th Company, 87th Signal) were also reconstituted at Ft. Irwin on June 1.

Sleepy little Ft. Irwin suddenly had a larger population than its commissary, post exchange, and available on-post family housing could handle. Groceries and other normal personal logistical needs required traveling some 35 miles through the desert to Barstow, CA, or even 75 miles farther from Ft. Irwin to George Air Force Base in Victorville, CA, during the next several months. The Army was not prepared to logistically support dependent families at Ft. Irwin. But a lot of memories were made while coping with this situation.

On June 1, the battalion's officer leadership consisted of Regular Army Lt. Col. Donald J. Majikas, who had served in the Korean War; an active-duty Reserve Maj. Thomas A. Batey, who was also a Korean War veteran; National Guard Maj. Louis A. Deering, who had been called to active duty only one week prior to the battalion's activation; a healthy mix of regular Army and active-duty Reserve captains; and four lieutenants, all of whom were recent OCS graduates. By mid-June, there were 17 lieutenants. None of the officers had previously worked together.

As luck would have it, I reported in the modest battalion headquarters while Lt. Col. Majikas and Maj. Batey were deep in conversation. I introduced myself and got straight to it. "Is this where I should sign in?"

"This will do," Lt. Col. Majikas said.

Both he and the major were very cordial and seemed pleased to welcome me to the battalion. After some small talk, I asked if job assignments had been determined. Lt. Col. Majikas said I was the last captain to arrive and that all the captain positions were filled except the battalion S-1 (adjutant). So, that would be my job. When I indicated that I wanted a firing battery, he responded that all the BC positions had been filled. I told him that all my time as a lieutenant had been in firing batteries, including commanding one for six months in which we conducted live-fire exercises each week. I knew field artillery techniques and procedures quite well. I'd had a lot of field artillery experience at every officer position in a firing battery. If we were going to war, I wanted a firing battery.

We went back and forth on this subject for a few more minutes. Finally, Lt. Col. Majikas asked me if I could see a particular office door from where we were standing. I answered, "Yes, sir."

"Well, that is your blankety-blank office, and you are the blankety-blank battalion S-1. Get your ass in that office and start learning your job," he snapped.

It was not exactly how I had hoped my first meeting with my new boss (and rater, I might add) would be conducted. I wondered if our relationship would erode even further in the future, if that was possible.

7th Battalion, 13th Artillery Headquarters, June 1, 1966, Fort Irwin CA, Mojave Desert, Photo provided by Col. Bill Collier.

The non-commissioned officer (NCO) leadership consisted of a well-qualified and experienced Battalion Sergeant Major Samuel R. McClure. He was a Marine during WWII and a soldier during the Korean War. Unfortunately, less than 1/4 of the authorized NCOs had reported by June 1, with only 75 percent of the NCOs on board when we deployed to Vietnam in October 1966. Even then, some 40 percent of these NCOs were one grade lower than the grade level their positions authorized.

Most of the second lieutenants were graduates of recent Officer Candidate classes at Ft. Sill, OK. More than 90 percent of the lower enlisted grades were draftees or volunteers who had recently graduated from Advance Individual Training cycles at Ft. Sill. At best, the battalion's personnel situation could be described as people new to the Army, unfamiliar with each other, and certainly not cognizant of the "teamwork" concept.

To further reveal the battalion's situation, every piece of equipment received during the four-month desert training period was a "hand-me-down"—mostly from National Guard and Army Reserve units, and usually in need of some maintenance. As I recall now, some equipment had been sitting at depot-level maintenance for years. All in all, it was a meager beginning for a unit being prepared for insertion into ongoing combat.

As for me, I was somewhat uncomfortable in the battalion headquarters for a week or so following my initial encounter with Lt. Col. Majikas. For the first couple of weeks in June, the battalion had only two or three jeeps and two trucks. Most officers were either not married, or their orders did not initially allow dependents to accompany them on reassignment to Ft. Irwin. I was in this latter category.

Transportation around Ft Irwin was difficult and time-consuming. People were frequently late getting places, causing progress to move at a snail's pace.

Lt. Col. Majikas drove his old 1954 green four-door Buick sedan to Ft. Irwin. He told me he would sell the car to "the officers" for $400 if they were interested. As it turns out, they were exceedingly interested. So, I collected donations to buy the car. It was taken to the motor pool, where it quickly and professionally became a convertible. Our unit crest, a red dragon, was stenciled on all four doors, the hood, and the trunk. From that point on, it was known as the "Dragon Wagon." Some days, as many as 12 or more officers were in (and on) the Dragon Wagon as we slowly made our way from the sleeping quarters to the battalion area each day. We used it quite frequently for battalion functions during the next three or four weeks.

Assignment orders were quickly amended to allow dependents to travel to Ft. Irwin. Availability of family quarters on Ft. Irwin was extremely limited. It was late June and early July before we saw families arriving and, with them, privately owned cars. Life in the desert was as new to the family members as it was to the soldiers, and the newly arrived women made a special effort to get to know each other as quickly as possible. Families had to travel to Barstow or towns even farther away for groceries each week.

Receipt of our authorized military vehicles and the arrival of families with their cars reduced the need for the Dragon Wagon after several more weeks. Soon, it was parked in front of the battalion headquarters—that is, when not being driven around Ft. Irwin by some officer simply having fun.

The battalion trained in the desert each week, and one day, I overheard the operations officer, Maj. Deering, talking with Lt. Col. Majikas in his office, since my office was next to his. The discussion concerned the observation post (OP): *Who was available to manage the OP and train/control the recently commissioned 2LTs during field (desert) training?* I quickly poked my head into the Lt. Col.'s office to remind him that I had been an FO on a weekly basis for 10 months in the artillery training base. Thus, I volunteered for the job and got it.

That sure was a lot easier than the first time I asked Lt. Col. Majikas for a specific job. I didn't get my butt chewed out, either!

When the battalion conducted training in the desert, I was the officer-in-charge of the OP. When not in the desert, I was the S-1/adjutant pushing paper and assigning incoming enlisted personnel, assisted by the new personnel warrant officer (WO) Takita.

Our 18 105-mm howitzers arrived on June 20. The commander of Ft. Irwin loaned the battalion trucks and other equipment from those stored for the training of Reserve and National Guard units. As our equipment arrived, the Ft. Irwin equipment was returned.

Training in the desert was quite an experience. It was difficult for us to understand how training in a hot, dry, and sandy desert offered any meaningful preparation for combat in a hot, wet jungle. However, later, in Vietnam, we understood. Three different locations were selected as OPs. Two were dark volcanic rock, and nothing else could be found in these locations. Our Jeeps carried two five-gallon metal cans—one for gasoline and the other for water. It was normal for a human to consume one or more gallons of water per day while sitting or standing on the OP and not be wet from perspiration. There were white salt lines under our arms and around our necks, but never any sweat.

On one occasion, I walked over to a rocky spot and sat down. After a few minutes of silence, one of the FOs asked: "What's going on, Captain?" I replied that I was taking a few minutes to cool off under this tree. There wasn't a tree anywhere for miles! The FOs had a good laugh about that.

Target identification was at a premium. There was simply a scarcity of reasonably identifiable objects in the impact area to call targets. Large single or clusters of black lava rocks and cactus plants that were less than two feet tall were the only targets in early June.

Second Lieutenant James Dower was assigned the task of procuring salvage yard-type trucks for placement in the impact area.

Lt. Dower was the battalion reconnaissance and survey officer. He was able to locate and transport 15 salvaged two-and-a-half-ton military trucks to Ft. Irwin. After painting each of them different colors, these disabled vehicles were placed throughout the wide-ranging and wide-open impact area. His survey section determined the grid coordinates (exact location) of each vehicle and also a couple of OPs. He provided me with their accurate grid coordinates. Knowing the grid coordinates of all these locations gave me credibility with the FOs.

Lt. Dower graduated from OCS with several of the other Second Lieutenants in the battalion. After a couple of weeks, these Second Lieutenants seemed to know the precise grid coordinates of most of the painted vehicles in the impact area. *I wonder how?* I had to be a bit more creative in target location from that point on.

Contrast this FO training in the desert with the jungles and mountains of Vietnam, with triple canopied forests and thick foliage that significantly limited visibility and observation. In Vietnam, FOs often had to decide which type of artillery round and fuse was needed for their initial adjustment round just to ensure the accuracy of their coordinates cited for the target.

Our FOs adapted well to the challenges of desert operations, as did the firing batteries and all sections of the battalion. Unit training was conducted at the battery level in the classroom until June 27, when the battalion moved to the "field" for battery level training.

Live fire training began on July 3, and battalion-level coordinated training began in July and continued until mid-August.

There was a brief interruption in our training. Several soldiers from a National Guard unit were reported missing and presumed lost in the desert around Ft. Irwin. The battalion conducted search operations throughout a large area of the desert around the post for a period of one week. Our FO teams traversed the area in jeeps, and our soldiers were deployed to various areas each day and essentially walked in the desert using a line formation, keeping in sight those on their right and left. Training resumed after a week. Search operations continued using other units and aircraft. As I recall, the soldiers were located at some point, but only after they had expired. This experience reinforced the need for preapproval for all trips to the desert for any reason.

The battalion responded well to great leadership from the battalion commander and his staff. We trained hard in the Mojave Desert from June through August. On August 18, the battalion conducted a live-fire exercise which was evaluated by personnel from Ft. Ord, CA. Upon successfully passing the evaluation, the battalion was declared "combat ready" and deemed qualified for deployment to Vietnam.

Normal live fire training in the U.S. required a designated safety officer to check the data on each gun before it could be considered safe to fire. We trained like we thought it would be in combat—with no safety officers available to check data. Consequently, each gun chief was held responsible for the accuracy and safety of procedures and data on his gun. It was good training. Upon arrival in Vietnam, our gun chiefs hit the ground, firing accurately and safely, so to speak.

With unit training and required individual training successfully completed, it was time to prepare our equipment for movement to the West Coast and loading onto a cargo vessel for further shipment to Vietnam. The battalion's still incomplete complement of authorized equipment continued to arrive throughout this movement period. All equipment was moved to Long Beach, CA, from September 19 to 29, 1966.

Second Lt. Terry R Lane and Cpl. James E. Vieland, both assigned to Alpha Battery, were designated as the only battalion personnel to accompany the equipment across the Pacific Ocean to Qui Nhon, Vietnam. Lt. Lane and Cpl. Vieland arrived at Long Beach, CA, on September 29. The merchant marine ship, the John C., arrived in Long Beach's harbor on September 30. The battalion's equipment loading process occurred October 1-4, 1966. Lt. Lane and Cpl. Vieland boarded the John C. on October 5.

All battalion personnel were given leave to visit and relocate families elsewhere while we would be in Vietnam. One last chore remained before going on leave. The battalion would conduct a direct-fire competition with all five batteries competing.

There is a collection of exceptionally large boulders called the "rockpile," a short distance from Ft. Irwin on the road to Barstow. Several National Guard and/or Reserve units had painted their unit crest on some of these rocks over the years. The 7th Battalion,

13th Artillery painted their red dragon unit crest on a prominent boulder in late September 1966.

Headquarters Battery and Service Battery each borrowed a howitzer from one of the firing batteries. The battalion commander suggested the target, and all officers agreed. It would be none other than the Dragon Wagon! The last Saturday morning at Ft. Irwin, before taking leave, families and quite a few other interested personnel gathered at a location near the "rockpile" for this contest. Remember, Ft. Irwin is in the middle of the Mojave Desert. Not many opportunities for entertainment. This contest was a big event!

Alpha Battery fired and missed the Dragon Wagon. Alpha Battery's crew and their families were disappointed. The rest of the spectators were yelling and hooting with joy. *Over a one-round miss? Really?* Bravo Battery prepared, fired, and missed. Improbable but not impossible. You could hear the crowd yelling all the way to Barstow! *Maybe.* Then, Charlie Battery's crew prepared to fire. They had gone to school on Alpha's and Bravo's attempts. They were ready. They were pumped. No way could they miss.

Charlie Battery fired and missed. *Wow!* The crowd noise greatly diminished. Surely, Headquarters Battery people and Service Battery were not adequately trained to conduct direct fire. Headquarters' personnel fired and hit the Dragon Wagon, then Service Battery fired and hit the Dragon Wagon. The second hit caused the Dragon Wagon's horn to start blowing continuously.

This direct fire shoot is now folklore. People failed to remember that most of Service Battery's personnel were trained cannoneers. A number of those in Headquarters were also trained cannoneers. My wife told me of a lady in the audience crying and saying how sad it was that the Dragon Wagon's horn blowing signified that the wagon did not want to die. All attendees and soldiers got into their vehicles and drove away to the sound of the Dragon Wagon's horn.

I agreed with that lady. It *was* sad.

Ft. Irwin became the U.S. Army's National Training Center (NTC) in 1980. Over the years, units training at the NTC painted their crests on one of the boulders in the rockpile. In 2015, on the way to a family reunion in California, I visited Ft. Irwin and stopped at the rockpile to look for the Red Dragon. The rockpile is now well-populated with unit crests. Happily, the red dragon is still there, albeit somewhat faded!

The battalion's personnel, minus our advance party, departed Ft. Irwin early the morning of October 7, 1966, enroute to San Diego. We were transported on numerous Army buses, similar to civilian school buses. It was an uncomfortable five-hour road trip. Upon arrival near the entrance to the naval base at San Diego, we were greeted by anti-war protesters. They were shouting mostly unintelligible words and some objects were thrown at our buses.

Some smaller but critical items of equipment arrived just days before we shipped. Several NCOs hand carried some of the equipment on board the USNS Charles Dodson Barrett (T-AP-196). I recall at least one gun chief had received his gun's panoramic telescope the day before departure and had to carry it with him across the Pacific Ocean and for two weeks in Vietnam until his howitzer arrived at Landing Zone (LZ) Hammond.

The advance party consisted of 36 personnel, including the battalion commander, the command sergeant major, all five battery commanders, and their first sergeants. Several NCOs in the battalion personnel section also traveled with the advance party. This group departed George Air Force Base, CA, on October 10, 1966, flying on a Lockheed C-130 Hercules four-engine turboprop military transport aircraft. They arrived in Qui Nhon, Vietnam, four days later after a layover in Hawaii to resolve an engine problem.

In Vietnam, the battalion was initially assigned to the 52nd Artillery Group, 1st Field Forces Vietnam. Their mission was enormous. In the early days of the troop unit build-up in Vietnam, procedures and the means to ensure a smooth and efficient reception for incoming units were not yet well developed. To enter the logistical system was a real chore. Preparations to off-load our equipment from the John C. and successfully transport the battalion's equipment to LZ Hammond would be a daunting task. The two weeks before the arrival of the battalion's soldiers and their equipment were busy, tense, and frustrating for the advance party.

The John C. sailed from Long Beach, CA, enroute to Qui Nhon, Vietnam, on October 6, 1966, with most all of the equipment of the 7th Battalion, 13th Artillery.

The USNS Barrett sailed from San Diego, CA, enroute to Qui Nhon, Vietnam, on October 8, 1966, with approximately 2,100 military personnel on board, including the soldiers of the 7th Battalion, 13th Artillery.

CHAPTER THREE
SAILING ACROSS THE PACIFIC OCEAN

I COULD NOT BELIEVE WHAT I WAS SEEING. The USNS Barrett was still well within clear vision of San Diego, CA, and the beautiful Naval Amphibious Base at Coronado.

A battalion of 500-plus U.S. Marines joined the Army contingent at San Diego.

Five military units, consisting of two field artillery battalions (7th Battalion, 9th Artillery, and the 7th Battalion, 13th Artillery), two signal companies (5th Company, 86th Battalion and 5th Company, 87th Battalion), and the Marine battalion, totaling approximately 2,100 military personnel on the ship going to Vietnam. All these units—except the battalion of Marines—were activated and had trained at Ft. Irwin. And I was now looking at perhaps 50 to 75 soon-to-be American fighting men leaning over the side of the ship, seasick already. As a Virginia boy who grew up on a large creek fed by a large river, such a sight was unfathomable. *What will they do when the ship gets further out into the Pacific Ocean with higher ocean waves?* Just wait!

A troop ship has limited entertainment opportunities, even for the ship's crew and officers. As I watched during the 20-day trip to Vietnam, sailing a ship the size of the Barrett required constant work and vigilance. The ship's crew was not interested in entertaining soldiers or Marines. Many of our military personnel found ways to keep themselves busy or stay otherwise occupied. Some read for hours on end. Others loved to talk and found other talkers with whom to bide their time. Many slept. For the first four or five days, many moaned and groaned and vomited due to seasickness. Gambling became a new hobby. Interestingly, some had never seriously gambled until this trip while others seemed to be professional gamblers disguised as soldiers. By the end of this voyage, many more would be well-experienced gamblers.

Each day was physical training (PT) day. Twice a day was the initial goal. For some unimaginable reason, the Marines and soldiers did not want to do PT together (or at the same time), even if separated on deck. They would rather fight each other as their means of PT. For a couple of days, we thought they would get over this mentality and settle down. *We thought wrong.*

The ship's crew had enough plywood needed to erect walls between the two services below deck. At least there was some peace at that location! Thereafter, the Marines would come topside for PT and return below while the Army was brought topside for their PT. When much smaller groups from each service were allowed topside, they left each other alone. Each service had men who needed more freedom to walk and roam than others. That is probably the only reason they behaved. This was the daily routine most of the 18 days it took to get to Okinawa, Japan, with some interruptions.

One major interruption occurred three or four days after we were underway. The officers and some senior NCOs from all five combat units were bunked in decent quarters topside. In the lobby was an electronic or magnetic map behind glass with a miniature ship that indicated the ship's location and direction. Many officers, including me, observed this map several times each day, noting that it had moved only slightly since we last checked it. Yes, we were that bored. It seemed that we were crossing the Pacific Ocean at a snail's pace in a westerly direction. Suddenly, one morning, perhaps October 12 or 13, the miniature ship was pointed north. *Why?*

The ship's captain posted a statement that we were going north to avoid as much of a typhoon named Kathy as possible.

But it was sunny. The seas seemed normal.

By nightfall, the good weather and calm seas were gone. The waves were larger as the rain became more intense. We were given orders to ensure all personnel were in their bunks and stayed there for the next 10 or so hours. This included all officers. They did not have to tell any of us twice. It was getting worrisome.

Soon, the waves were over 30 feet high. My cabin had a porthole, and I could see us dip below the waves. The ship would go up a wave, and as it went over the wave's top and turned downward, the ship's propeller, called the screw, would come out of the water, making a clearly audible sound. As the ship went down the other side of the wave, the screw re-entered the water again, making a different but clearly audible sound. To my imagination, the ship seemed to teeter and shake on top of each wave. There was no doubt in my mind that this ship was eventually going to crack open and, well… you know what I was thinking.

Later in Vietnam, I was in a couple of big battles. In battle, you still have some freedom of movement and the ability to make decisions that can influence the situation. On the USNS Barrett, I was more scared riding out Typhoon Kathy for several hours than I was in future Vietnam battles. Simply stated, I had no freedom of movement outside of my bunk, on which I maintained a constant death grip, and I clearly had no means or authority to make any command decisions. I had no control over that typhoon or its impact on the ship whatsoever!

My soldiers told nightmarish stories of being in the hold of the ship where some 2,000-plus men were stacked vertically 4 bunks high. It was *hot* in the troops' sleeping compartments. At this point, I will leave it to your imagination what adverse conditions existed with seasick men in hot, crowded sleeping compartments. It was not pleasant. Today, we laugh about this experience. However, it was not laughable in October 1966.

As you have likely put together, somehow, we survived Typhoon Kathy and sailed on toward Okinawa. On or about October 16, 1966, at some point in the middle of the Pacific Ocean, we crossed the 180th meridian, better known as the International Date Line (IDL). If you go west of this line, you advance into the next day. If you are going east when crossing this line, you return to the previous day. People crossing the IDL for the first time on a ship were subjected to a fun initiation. I was initiated in March 1963 enroute by ship to Korea, and I have the card to prove it. Only a small number of us on the Barrett had such cards. With assistance from several of the ship's crew, we conducted this memorable initiation on the Barrett and issued each soldier and Marine his card, verifying his initiation into the "Domain of the Golden Dragon."

A memorable initiation while crossing the 180th Meridian (International Date Line) on October 16, 1966. Photo provided by Col. Bill Collier.

Upon successful initiation, each soldier, sailor, and Marine earned a personal "Domain of the Golden Dragon" card.

U. S. Army soldiers and U.S. Marines aboard the USNS Barrett relaxing and enjoying a view of the Pacific Ocean.

To the best of my memory, after 18 days on the ocean, the USNS Barrett arrived the morning of October 25, 1966, at Naval Base White Beach, Okinawa. The ship tied up at a dock known as "the long pier." We were the only ship moored at this long pier that day. Around noon, most troops were given a 12-hour pass requiring them to return no later than midnight.

Oh boy! Eighteen days on the Pacific Ocean and now twelve hours on a Naval base. Perhaps everyone would try to catch a movie or just relax and stretch their legs?

The battalion surgeon, Capt. James A. Edmond, M.D., and I took a taxi into the city of Uruma, Okinawa, to find a restaurant. There was not much to see and very little happening in those days. So, we returned to the Naval base and sought out the Naval Base officers' club for food and drinks. Little did we know what was really happening at White Beach.

I was the officer of the day (OD) that night. We returned to the ship a little before 2300 hours. All was quiet. Dr. Edmond joined me on the deck immediately above the wide gangplank that personnel used to depart and return to the ship. Roll call was not planned that evening. We simply hoped everyone would return safely and on time.

It seemed that all 2,100 troops decided to return to the ship starting around 2330 hours. Half (or more) of them were clearly extremely intoxicated. It was quite the sight to see so many of them staggering on the long pier. It was very entertaining. Suddenly, we observed a gray-panel Navy pickup truck approaching the long pier at a higher-than-expected speed. The cargo section of the pickup was packed with soldiers and Marines intending to return to the ship. Unfortunately, as the driver approached the beginning of the long pier, he missed it and plowed into the water. Of course, this caused the truck to stop quickly. The doctor and I watched many people that did not stop with the truck suddenly, flying through the air and landing in the water.

"You're going to be busy tonight!" I told the doctor. To this day, it still boggles my mind that there were only minor injuries from this incident.

Many comical incidents occurred as our soldiers and Marines returned to the ship. Even though the gangplank was 10-to-15 feet wide, several individuals came close to falling off into the water. Several swam from the shore to the ship and attempted to gain entrance by climbing the huge anchor chain. Of course, they were unable to succeed.

The duty officer lieutenant suffered a lot of harassment that evening. One tall, skinny, drunken soldier even accused him of stealing his watch and attempted to manhandle the lieutenant. I ordered that individual be thrown in the ship's brig. Lucky for him, another lieutenant quickly told me that the drunk soldier was in our battalion and requested to take him under his care instead. So be it.

In 2010, I met the drunk soldier at our battalion's first reunion in Chattanooga, TN. During the dinner, four couples seated together began reminiscing and telling stories about sailing across the Pacific Ocean. Donald Fernstrom recited the incident of almost being thrown in the ship's brig at White Beach. I quickly exclaimed, "You were that tall skinny soldier?" After Vietnam, Don went to college and law school. He became a successful civilian lawyer. By the way, he has an interesting story about why he was drunk that night. You will have to ask him personally for the details.

Our ship was scheduled to sail early in the morning. Sometime after midnight, a Navy lieutenant commander came aboard. Apparently, our soldiers and Marines had caused some trouble in one of the enlisted clubs on the base. I never did learn which ones specifically. The Navy club had a band playing while sailors, soldiers, and Marines were drinking and enjoying themselves. Rumor has it that some hours later in the evening, a sailor took the microphone and made disparaging remarks about the soldiers on the ship docked at the long pier. A Marine took offense at this and punched the sailor. A fight ensued with the Army and Marines fighting the Navy. Some said they eventually just began hitting anyone near them. Perhaps it's more accurate to say the fight evolved into a free-for-all.

The Navy lieutenant commander listed some "alleged" results of this melee, which included broken chairs and glasses, destroyed French doors, and a baby grand piano thrown into the pool. The lieutenant commander said the bill was around $9,000. So, we started taking up a collection. After an hour, it was obvious that we were having difficulty getting $1,000. I shared this with the lieutenant commander, who said that we either had to pay the full amount or the ship would not sail. Several soldiers heard his comment. They started chanting, "Ooooh, if we do not pay, then the ship does not set sail. They can't send us to Vietnam." Soon, hundreds of soldiers were chanting those words. I provided the lieutenant commander my sincerest smile and said that we would be glad to remain on Okinawa. He took the almost $1,000 and stomped off the ship. We sailed several hours later as scheduled.

From the Okinawa event, we surmised that the soldiers and Marines were now getting along. Finally! The next day we brought both services together for PT, but the hoped-for truce did not last. In less than 15 minutes, the bickering began anew. The Army was quickly removed from the open deck until the Marines' PT session was completed.

Several days later, on October 27, we arrived off the coast of Vietnam. The ship traveled north to the harbor at Da Nang, where the Marines were to disembark. As the ship traveled northward up the coast of Vietnam, the sounds of artillery were frequently heard. Helicopters were around, and close air support jet aircraft were seen dropping their ordnance. It was obvious that a war was occurring. Soldiers and Marines were on deck watching and listening to this for several hours. As the Marines began disembarking, the unexpected happened—again. The soldiers and Marines who had picked fights with each other all the way across the Pacific Ocean were now hugging, some with tears in their eyes as they wished each other well. It was mystifying. Maybe they were all blood brothers or first cousins, and we just did not realize it until that moment!

After the Marines had disembarked, the ship turned south that evening as it sailed towards Qui Nhon. The night was often lit up with illumination rounds and airburst artillery. Depending on their distance from us, you could hear the *boom, boom* of artillery being fired and impacting somewhere. All the soldiers were on deck and watched this go on for hours. Everyone watched and listened but did not speak. These sights and sounds had everyone's attention. It was our second realization and confirmation that a war was actually occurring, and we soon would be participating.

We dropped anchor just north of Qui Nhon harbor on October 28. At daylight, a hole was opened in the side of the Barrett about halfway down. A large rope ladder was thrown over the side. As a young boy in the late 1940s and the 1950s, I had watched so many John Wayne and other World War II movies that I knew exactly what to expect next. Sure enough, several amphibious landing craft arrived about an hour later. We climbed out the large hole and down the rope ladder into the landing craft, rolling with the waves. From there, it was a short ride to a sandy beach.

Arrival at a sandy beach, slightly north of Qui Nhon, South Vietnam, October 28, 1966. Photo by U.S. Army Photo Section, 54th Signal Battalion.

After traveling from the USNS Barrett to a sandy beach north of Qui Nhon on October 29, 1966, we were staged for this arrival picture before we could offload onto the beach. I am in the second row wearing sunglasses. The battalion doctor, Capt. James Edmond, is on my right.

At this point, I have to admit that the watercraft that ferried us from the USNS Barrett offshore Qui Nhon harbor to a nearby, seemingly uninhabited sandy beach did not look like the Landing Ship Tanks (LSTs) I had seen in all the old World War II movies. In the year 2021, I proudly showed the pictures of several of the watercraft after they arrived on the sandy beach to my good friend Jim Null, a retired Navy master chief petty officer. This was as if to say to him that I had some experience with Navy vessels, too. He smiled and politely said that it was not an LST. It was not even a Navy vessel. Then he "messed" with me some more by saying that it had wheels and that the Navy would never put wheels on their watercraft. *He is enjoying this*, I thought.

"The vessel you showed me a picture of is most likely a LARC (Lighter Amphibious Resupply Cargo) Army watercraft with wheels," he said. We had a good laugh.

The Army *did* have watercraft at the time, and still does.

Our individual rifles and pistols accompanied us in the ship's cargo hold on the Barrett as we crossed the Pacific Ocean. The weapons were retrieved from the hold and issued to us before we climbed down the rope ladder onto the watercraft, aka the LARC.

Ammunition was not issued. What if we were attacked approaching the beach? Or even worse, attacked as we were taking the beach? Not a good scenario. We were armed with our .45 caliber pistols and M-14 rifles. But, again, no ammunition. Many soldiers were yelling, "Where is the ammo?" We were fearful that as soon as we landed on the beach, the North Vietnamese Army (NVA) soldiers would start firing at us.

Indeed, as we landed on the beach, we were being shot at. Several photographers were there "shooting" pictures of our arrival.

Our battalion commander, Lt. Col. Majikas, Com. Sgt. Maj. (CSM) McClure, and several others were there to welcome us to Vietnam. We were loaded onto two-and-a-half-ton trucks and convoyed to LZ Hammond 30-plus miles north of Qui Nhon, where we entered the war.

MERCHANT MARINE SHIP JOHN C.

The heavily loaded merchant marine ship John C. departed Long Beach on October 6, 1966. On October 16, the John C. encountered the tail end of Typhoon Kathy with 100-mile-per-hour winds and waves so high that water came over the bow of the ship, preventing personnel from going on deck from October 14 to 16, 1966. Lt. Lane and Cpl. Vieland related that while lying in bed, they too were very concerned when the ship would lift out of the water and slam back into the ocean, sending vibrations through the ship. They also said they were expecting the ship to break in half.

The John C.'s captain received a message that the Qui Nhon, Vietnam harbor was too busy to handle them as scheduled. Consequently, the ship was diverted to the Manila harbor in the Philippines, which would delay their arrival in Qui Nhon. The ship arrived in Manila on October 25. During refueling operations, Cpl. Vieland told me he witnessed two merchant marine sailors jump from the John C. into the Manila harbor, wherein they swam to shore. He did not know if they ever returned to the ship or not. The John C. departed for Qui Nhon on October 27, arriving at the harbor on the 29th.

The ship was scheduled to be the first one unloaded at a new dock. However, all nine docks were occupied by other ships. Therefore, unloading began out in the harbor on November 2 but was stopped on November 5 due to rough seas. Unloading resumed on November 8.

The last piece of equipment, a jeep, was unloaded at 1000 hours on November 10, 1966. As the crane lifted the jeep from the ship's hold into the air and rotated it to a nearby barge, the jeep had a personal escort, Lt. Lane, sitting in the driver's seat! Lt. Lane and Cpl. Vieland traveled with the battalion's equipment to LZ Hammond, where they rejoined their unit, Alpha Battery, 7th Battalion, 13th Artillery, and entered the war.

Little did I know at that time that I would become the Alpha Battery commander and that Lt. Lane would be one of my forward observers. And he survived a full year as a FO in combat, thankfully. Cpl. Vieland proved himself to be an outstanding soldier and leader. In a firing battery, the base piece, usually gun number three, has the best howitzer section and fires all registrations and fire mission adjustments. Based on his performance and demonstrated potential, I promoted Cpl. Vieland to sergeant and later to acting gun chief of the base piece.

THE BATTALION'S ADVANCE PARTY

The advance party departed from George Air Force Base, CA, on October 10, 1966, and, after a refueling and engine repair stop in Hawaii, arrived in Vietnam on October 14. I later learned that their mission was a daunting task. Those of us taking the equipment or troop cruise ships across the Pacific Ocean were able to kick back and enjoy three leisurely, uneventful weeks of seagoing fun as previously described. The advance party has a different memory of those same three weeks in October.

Led by the battalion commander, the 36 members of the advance party entered a largely chaotic situation. Their missions included ensuring in-country combat and support units were aware of the battalion's impending arrival, making a myriad of preparations and coordinating their troop and equipment arrivals and subsequent disposition, establishing geographical locations for all elements of the battalion, and energizing the already overburdened logistical system to integrate yet another battalion into their system. The 1st Battalion, 30th Artillery was the host unit for our battalion and was primarily responsible for initially erecting temporary billeting and messing facilities.

Although members of the advance party technically entered the war on October 14, their efforts could more accurately be considered administrative until the USNS Barrett and the John C. arrived. The battalion's personnel and equipment were fully deployed to LZ Hammond by November 10.

CHAPTER FOUR
ENTERING THE WAR

T HE 7TH BATTALION, 13th Artillery crossed the Pacific Ocean on the USNS Barrett and arrived safe and sound in Vietnam on October 28, 1966. The objective was to remain safe and sound as we entered a completely foreign and unfamiliar environment while, every moment, we expected a battle to erupt. We eventually realized that this war was, and would continue to be, different from the WWII and Korean War Hollywood movies we had watched during our childhood days. From the time we arrived on the beach north of Qui Nhon, it was satisfying to watch how our American troops adapted to new and varying circumstances.

Without any ammunition, everyone was anxious on the road trip north to the place referred to only as LZ Hammond. Fear of the unknown was clearly present. Even so, the trip was uneventful. LZ Hammond was still under development. Our host unit was the 1st Battalion, 30th Artillery (a 155 mm howitzer artillery battalion). This battalion had assisted our advance party in preparing our location on the north end of LZ Hammond.

The airstrip on LZ Hammond was not level and had a higher elevation at the north end than the other. The airstrip had what appeared to be some sort of oil sprayed on its surface and then pierce steel planking (PSP) on top of that instead of concrete. For the first week on LZ Hammond, we were convinced that the

C-130 Hercules aircraft would not gain enough speed to allow launch before running out of airstrip. Somehow, they always took off safely with their four engines giving it everything they had.

Why was this a point of interest? Perhaps this is due to the fact that most of the battalion's assigned area was at the end of the airstrip, including that of the service battery. I felt as if I could jump up and touch the plane's belly as it lifted off the ground. This was incredibly worrisome in the beginning. After a few weeks, the landings and departures of the planes seemed routine and normal.

Headquarters and Headquarters Battery had more officers than the other batteries. Initially, our sleeping quarters were general-purpose medium tents erected by our host unit just slightly to the side of the airstrip and on soft and somewhat sandy soil. The floors were made of 105 mm ammunition boxes. This was monsoon season. During our third or fourth night at LZ Hammond, heavy rains occurred. Our general-purpose medium tents started to collapse in certain areas. All the officers jumped up and ran outside to hold onto the rope guidelines and poles to prevent further collapse until help arrived to add more stability using sandbags. I was holding a guideline. Capt. David Taylor, our assistant operations officer, was holding one next to mine. We were wearing only a steel helmet on our head, an undershirt that was recently dyed brown, underpants, and unlaced black boots. We looked at each other and started laughing uncontrollably. David said, "This is one hell of a way to fight a war!"

Two days after arriving on LZ Hammond, Lt. Col. Majikas told me, without any further explanation, that I was now the Service Battery commander. Service Battery provides all classes of supplies to the battalion. I immediately told him that I was not a trained logistician and had no desire to become one. I really wanted a firing battery. He put his hand up as to signal me to be quiet and said something like, "We are not going to have *another* conversation similar to what we had at Ft. Irwin, are we?"

Of course, that ended *that* conversation.

In 1966, additional military units were arriving in Vietnam on a regular basis. The buildup was in full swing. The Army's logistical system was being pushed to its limits. Vietnamese nationals were also being employed at various levels throughout our supply system. That was a good thing at times and a disaster at others. If you were hard-pressed for a particular item, you had to go to Qui Nhon and work the system yourself. Otherwise, it was a coin toss on when you might get what you had requisitioned and needed.

Service Battery had a chief warrant officer (CWO), Gennaro A. Picardo. He was an NCO during the Korean War and had since become a warrant officer. He was pure gold for us. He had detailed knowledge of the supply system, lots of patience, and charisma. Chief Picardo had been on the battalion's advance party and had played a major role in preparing the requisitions for all classes of supply our battalion needed to get us started sufficiently.

The requisitions had been forwarded up the line similar to how it was done in the U.S. It seemed that the requisitions were being filled and shipped to LZ Hammond on a trickle-down basis rather than in the quantities needed for the soon-to-be-arriving battalion. Chief Picardo had asked for permission to go to Qui Nhon to ensure the battalion was properly established in the system before I assumed command. He made the same request to me. I explained to the Chief that I was more comfortable shooting artillery than requisitioning supplies and promptly approved his request. He spent three days in Qui Nhon, and like magic, our supply system began functioning as it should.

For the next three months, I performed as the service battery commander. With CWO Picardo and two very good soldiers of his choosing, my job was easy, and the logistical mission of the battalion operated as designed. All of the credit for our success goes to CWO Picardo, Specialist 4 Terry Stephenson, and another soldier whose name escapes me.

All five batteries were co-located at LZ Hammond in October, and probably November as well. Headquarters and Headquarters Battery and Service Battery remained on LZ Hammond during this time. The firing batteries were given missions to support the various First Cavalry Division (Airmobile) brigades throughout the First Cav's Area of Operations in Military Region II (MR II), the 173rd Airborne Brigade, the First Capital Republic of Korea (Tiger) Division, and the regular and irregular military forces of the Army of South Vietnam. These fire-support missions often required the firing batteries to relocate from time to time. The battalion's initial mission was to support the First Capital Republic of Korea (Tiger) Division in Operation Meng Ho (Fierce Tigers) 7 beginning November 11. On January 5, 1967, the battalion was detached from the 52nd Artillery Group and attached to the First Field Force Vietnam (IFFV) Artillery.

ALPHA BATTERY COMMANDER

Lt. Col. Majikas conducted a staff call on LZ Hammond, especially when two or all three of the firing batteries had returned. At the conclusion of a staff call the first week of February 1967, he asked me if I still wanted to become a Regular Army (RA) officer. I answered in the affirmative. He then told me to stand up, raise my right hand, and take the oath. After swearing me in as an RA officer, he told everyone to return to their batteries.

I started out of the tent heading in the direction of Service Battery when Lt. Col. Majikas yelled: "Where are you going, Collier?" I replied that I was going to my battery. He said that I was going in the wrong direction and pointed in the direction I should be going. Then, with a big smile and a handshake, he said, "You wanted a firing battery, and you are now the Alpha Battery commander, effective right now." After five months as the battalion adjutant and four months as the Service Battery commander, I finally got a firing battery.

I was ecstatic. What a great day!

I then had to reorient my mind from logistical support for my battalion to artillery support for the 1st Air Cavalry Division (as it was known at that time) during Operations Thayer II and Pershing. Alpha Battery was operational control (OPCON) to the 1st Air Cavalry with a mission of general support at LZ Hammond. I was told later that the battalion was now attached to the 1st Air Cavalry Division artillery.

Two days later, on February 6, Alpha Battery received orders to travel south for a mission involving the defense of Qui Nhon. The First Capital Republic of Korea (Tiger) Division was responsible for a portion of the Qui Nhon outer perimeter. This was the same division that provided me comfort in South Korea in 1964 when I attempted to perform duties as an artillery liaison officer during a joint exercise between the First Cavalry Division and the Tiger Division. Talk about going full circle. The Tiger Division had requested additional artillery support from the Americans to help them with their defense of the Qui Nhon mission.

Alpha Battery conducted a road march southward on Highway 1 for some 20-30 miles before turning eastward onto single-lane dirt roads. Our designated position was an established artillery position halfway up the side of a small mountain. A small stream ran down the mountain on the east side of this position. Within one week, battery personnel had pieced together six 105 mm howitzer fiber containers in order to capture water from the stream for use as a shower. The men constructed a floor and towel hanging racks from the wooden crates used to transport two 105 mm rounds in fiber containers. The water was clear but cold. My troops seemed to enjoy this makeshift shower to the fullest. I know that I did. It seemed that someone was always using it, especially during the hottest part of the day.

An outdoor shower located near a Korean artillery position in Thuy Phuoc District near Qui Nhon. The nearby mountain stream provided continuous water. Alpha Battery, 7th Battalion, 13th Artillery improved shower amenities, February 1967. Photo provided by Col. Bill Collier.

An Alpha Battery, 7th Battalion, 13th Artillery howitzer located in the South Korean position near Qui Nhon, South Vietnam, February-March 1967. Photo provided by Col. Bill Collier.

Our mess sergeant, Staff Sergeant Haynie, decided to take a two-and-a-half-ton truck pulling a water trailer into Qui Nhon to get us some fresh meat, vegetables, eggs, water, and milk if possible. Everyone was looking forward to his venture. Upon his return that afternoon, his truck had numerous bullet holes in it. He swore he'd never make that trip again.

It just so happened that the South Korean infantry company commander that we were supporting was visiting me at that time. He was fluent in English and heard Haynie's ranting and raving. After speaking to his driver in Korean, his driver quickly departed my location, returning in 30 minutes. He brought metal picture plaques of the Tiger Division's mascot. The captain told me to have them placed on the front, rear, and both sides of the mess truck. *Staff Sergeant Haynie should not have any more trouble*, we thought. After some serious coaxing, we finally convinced Haynie to make another Qui Nhon run. It seems that the Viet Cong were extremely afraid of the Tiger Division. Staff Sergeant Haynie made three trips per week to Qui Nhon for the next five weeks without incident. The metal pictures of a ferocious tiger on his mess truck served to give him safe passage.

Captain Bill Collier, a South Korean Tiger Division Infantry company commander and his driver observing enemy locations from South Korean Artillery position north of Qui Nhon, February 8, 1967. Photo provided by Col. Bill Collier.

The day before Easter, March 25, 1967, had been a busy day for the battery with numerous requests for fire support. Four hours after the last mission was fired that evening, our battalion fire direction center notified us that we had fired an error, which had landed in a village, causing injuries to several local people.

An incident like this is an artillery battery commander's worst nightmare. Besides the harm to humans we may have caused, my thoughts were that after only seven weeks in command, I would be relieved. That was the usual outcome for these types of incidents.

Normal procedure was to determine what caused the error. I personally checked all six guns and could not find any discrepancies whatsoever. Then I looked to the battery fire direction center for answers. All seemed in order there, too. *Time to dig deeper to discover what caused the error*, I thought. Apparently, it was not a common or obvious error. When examining the target coordinates requested by the FO, it was clear that our missions were not even close to the village that was hit. We checked for wrong powder charge errors and 100 mil. quadrant and deflection errors in FDC or on the guns. I concluded that it was impossible for Alpha Battery to have fired into that village. It was now past midnight and early Easter morning.

Why couldn't I find the reason for the error? I wrestled with that thought most of the night. In reality, my cannoneers and fire direction computers had been computing and shooting artillery as a team in Vietnam since November 9, 1966. That was almost five months, and they had done so without an error. I had only watched them for seven weeks as their commander, but they were an outstanding battery when I inherited them, and they still were. So why the error? I finally concluded that Alpha Battery did not fire an error.

But how could I prove that they didn't?

At sunrise, I explained my conclusion to the battery formation and said I was going to that village, located almost due north of our battery position, to see for myself. It was located on the other side of a small river—possibly too deep for jeeps to ford—and was completely in Viet Cong-controlled territory. I intended to take two jeeps, one with a mounted machine gun. But I needed two volunteer drivers and one NCO.

I was concerned that maybe no one would volunteer. I had been their commander for only seven weeks, and I knew they held their previous commander in high regard. Besides, this was a somewhat harebrained thing to do, and only *my* butt was in danger of punishment if the battery had fired this error.

When I asked for volunteers, the response was overwhelming. I could not believe it. It seemed that almost everyone wanted to go. First Sergeant Robert Russell said he was going, followed by my driver, William Ziedler. I cannot recall the name of the other driver but I still remember his face.

As we traveled north toward the village, I began to doubt what I was doing. All of us could be killed. I should have asked the Korean company commander to have his troops accompany us. Too late for that now. I was so close to turning around when suddenly there we were at the river. No choice but to continue the mission.

As we had surmised earlier, the river was too deep for the jeeps to cross. I told the others to stay with the vehicles as I strapped on the M2 Aiming Circle. Map in hand, I waded across the river. Halfway across, I looked back. Russell and private first class (PFC) Zeidler were only a few yards behind me. That left a single driver with two jeeps and a machine gun. I noted that he had already turned the jeeps around as if prepared for a quick getaway. I smiled, thinking there would be a fat chance of a quick getaway if it came to it.

As the three of us entered the village, we drew a crowd. The villagers seemed to know why we were there and showed me the crater the round had made. I conducted a crater analysis which included a back azimuth, which clearly revealed the azimuth of fire of the gun that fired the round. While doing this analysis, a villager gave us several pieces of shrapnel. One piece had 155 mm on it. All the pieces were thicker than 105 mm ammo. With a lot of bowing and smiling, we got out of the village as fast as we could before any demands could be placed on us. Happy and relieved to be safely back in the battery position, I reported my findings to the battalion, and the real culprit was quickly identified. The shrapnel was picked up from me the next day, and Alpha Battery was no longer charged with the firing error.

All is well that ends well, as the saying goes. However, the ending could have been *very* different if things had not gone well in the village.

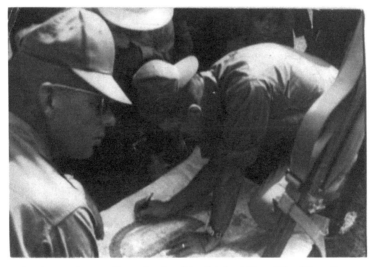

Behind enemy lines on Easter Sunday, March 26, 1967, in Thuy Phuoc District, Binh Dinh Province, Vietnam. Crater analysis being conducted by Capt. Collier with hat on backward. First Sergeant Robert Russell observing. PFC William Zeidler took the picture. In and out of the village in less than two hours before being discovered by the Viet Cong. Photo provided by Col. Bill Collier.

On April 3, Alpha Battery's mission was changed to operational control to the 1st Cavalry Division. We were directed to return to LZ Hammond. *On the road again.* Traveling on roads with a large contingency such as a firing battery is not my cup of tea. There were too many unknowns and potential dangers along the way. It was our first time on most of the roads we traveled in Vietnam, and they were therefore unfamiliar to us. For road marches, the improvised explosive devices (IED), snipers, and youths tossing hand grenades when traveling alongside roadside structures were my gravest concerns. The IEDs in Vietnam were not as sophisticated as those later seen in Iraq and Afghanistan, but they were every bit as deadly.

We began the march towards LZ Hammond on April 4. Enroute, we received coordinates of a different destination, taking us further north of LZ Hammond. Near dusk, we received new instructions to remain overnight at a location called LZ Two Bits. LZ Two Bits was just off the west side of Highway 1 in a small flat area surrounded by several small mountains and a fairly elevated, heavily treed ridge running mostly east and west. The area appeared peaceful. Everyone was ready to get off their vehicles and stretch their legs. It had been a long day.

The position was a previously established artillery position, although not one I would be proud to say Alpha Battery had established. Overhead cover was minimal. Either the executive officer, Second Lt. Bill Niess, or Sergeant First Class (SFC) Arturo Garcia, the Chief of the Firing Battery, laid the battery for direction. Garcia and I discussed the perimeter defense, which he was responsible for establishing that night. Charlie Battery, 7th Battalion, 13th Artillery was just up the road on the east side of Highway 1 at LZ Uplift. I think everyone was ready and hoping for a quiet night. I was pleased that we had arrived without incident.

We received a couple of fire missions around 2100 hours and fired them shortly after receipt. Sometime later, several incoming mortars landed. Two soldiers were lightly wounded. One of our perimeter outpost machine guns opened up on someone or something. Noise or movement near the perimeter was often found to be water buffalo, monkeys, or Viet Cong. Most perimeter guys would panic somewhat and start firing short bursts. I was not sure whether we were probed or *not* probed.

The next morning, two M42 Dusters, ostensibly like those used in World War II equipped with mobile tracked air-defense guns, arrived unexpectedly. The NCO in charge of each Duster asked if we had something to eat. While eating, my troops told them of the mortars the night before. Everyone thought the mortars were fired from the east-west ridge. I never knew their parent unit, yet they agreed to spend the day and night with us and return fire if we were mortared again. Of course, I welcomed them and their twin 40s. That night, instead of waiting for incoming mortars, the Dusters fired at different locations up and down the ridge and at different times throughout the night. We loved it. What a great sound they made. You have to be an artilleryman to appreciate that. Thankfully, we did not receive incoming mortars that night.

Several days later, we were on the road again to a place that became known as LZ English. A fair number of missions were fired from LZ English and other nearby locations during the remainder of April 1967 as the First Cav began making inroads throughout the Bong Son flatlands and into the mountainous An Loa Valley area. Most of our fire missions were normal textbook battery hasty and deliberate occupations by motor vehicles up-and-down Highway 1 between Qui Nhon and Bong Son.

On May 1, Lt. Col. Majikas informed me that Alpha Battery was going airmobile. The howitzers were too heavy for the Chinooks to lift in the high heat and humidity of Vietnam, especially in higher altitudes in the Central Highlands. To reduce weight, all 105-mm howitzer protective shields had to be removed. This was done in one day. To us, the howitzer looked weird without the shields. Weeks later, we thought they would look weird if the shields were replaced. Several 1st Cavalry Division NCOs spent that day and evening teaching combat air-assault techniques and procedures to the Alpha Battery NCOs.

Lt. Col. Majikas told me that the 3rd Brigade of the First Cavalry Division was planning to extend operations into the An Loa Valley, initially establishing a temporary forward tactical operations center (TOC) on a mountaintop to be named LZ Sandra. This location would be northwest of LZ English by approximately nine miles. A 105-mm Howitzer battery was scheduled to be co-located with the Brigade's forward TOC. Allegedly the 1st Battalion, 21st Artillery was their organic direct support battalion. Their Alpha Battery was tapped for the mission but was still engaged in an existing mission. The Division Artillery commander, Col. George W. Putnam, asked Lt. Col. Majikas if he had a battery available for this mission. Majikas passed the mission to his Alpha Battery. And we had one day to get ready.

On May 2, 1967, we lifted off LZ English for our first airmobile operation enroute to LZ Sandra. The mission—general support reinforcing the 1st Battalion, 21st Artillery—was for only two to four days, after which we would be replaced by the 3rd Brigade's organic artillery. We began receiving fire missions almost as the guns were arriving. It turned out to be a very busy four days in a target-rich environment.

Alpha Battery, 7th Battalion, 13th Artillery lifting off LZ English enroute to LZ Sandra, May 2, 1967. Photo provided by Col. Bill Collier.

LZ Sandra: A well-developed artillery position by August 1967. Note several howitzer positions, cannoneers, and the mess hall built by our cannoneers out of ammo boxes and other scrounged items. The 1st Cavalry Division Artillery Commander, Col. Putnam, said this was the best artillery position in the Division's area of operations. Of course, we had to agree with him!

The fact that all the terrain around us seemed to be sloping down in elevation did not escape notice by my troops. We were told at some point that LZ Sandra was the second-highest peak in the Central Highlands. At night, it got chilly up there. Some nights it actually got cold, especially with drizzle or rain. This was supposed to be a jungle warfare environment. Not so on LZ Sandra. The hot steamy jungle and lowlands were an environment we did not miss. But on cold nights, we did.

Sunrises on Sandra were simply glorious. Most mornings, the air around and above us was clear and fresh, while just below us there was nothing but white clouds. These clouds would usually burn off by 0800 or 0900 hours. Then you could look eastward and see the beautiful South China Sea with a lot of terrain between us and the sea. To the west, the mountainous Central Highlands were also beautiful. It was difficult to imagine a war was ongoing or that a North Vietnamese Division or two might actually be within that magnificent landscape. As it turned out, they were there.

We felt safer on Sandra than we did on the Bong Son Plains. Two sides of the mountain were fairly steep, one not quite as steep but which allowed several hundred yards of open fields if someone attempted to approach, and the fourth side would be more difficult to defend. The forward Cavalry Tactical Operations Center (TOC) was on that side and had a platoon or more of 7th Cavalry infantrymen on that perimeter. There was no reason to worry or be concerned. As I looked westward from Sandra, we seemed to be on the highest peak.

Artillery thrives on its ability to shoot, move, and communicate. On LZ Sandra, we probably had more opportunities to shoot and communicate than most artillery units in our area at that time. Most of my cannoneers could do any job on the guns equally well to include being the section chief. The same thing held true for the fire direction center. They were smart young men, highly trained, and motivated to accurately compute and develop fire commands.

However, I remained concerned that, by being so static on Sandra these many months, we might have lost some of our expertise and ability to move. I often wondered how that went when they finally came off LZ Sandra after I had departed Vietnam.

Of particular note was the battery's "First Artillery Raid." I received a message in mid-to-late May 1967 that Alpha Battery would conduct an artillery raid the next day. We were instructed to take four of our six howitzers, which we lovingly called "our guns," leaving the other two on LZ Sandra. We were told that approximately 300 105-mm rounds would be provided. The extent of the information provided us was limited to nothing more than this would be a "day trip." The XO, the FDO, Second Lt. Sam Harris and I did some fast planning and decided that the XO would stay with the two guns remaining on LZ Sandra.

The next morning, the weather was clear and warm with beautiful blue skies. Without incident, we lifted off Sandra with four howitzers, each slung under a Chinook helicopter and several other Chinooks with our cannoneers and fire direction personnel onboard.

The CFB, FDO, and I left several minutes earlier on a Huey helicopter. The flying time was approximately 25 to 30 minutes as we traveled further into the North Vietnamese-controlled Central Highlands in an approximate north-northwest direction. The scenery was gorgeous—mostly mountain ranges of varying heights. I was trying diligently to follow our travels on my topographical map but it was difficult, since the mountainous terrain basically looked the same. Glancing at Lt. Harris, I noted that he also was following our travel on his map. I was relieved. Harris was an OCS-commissioned officer with nine years prior enlisted service as a fire direction computer. Consequently, he was an outstanding Fire Direction Officer (FDO).

We landed on a high but thin mountain ridge. Normally, gun guides would accompany the advance party. With only four guns, the three of us traveling on the Huey would perform that function. With such a thin ridge, we decided to use a line formation for gun emplacement. Within minutes of our arrival, the guns arrived and were quickly dug in and laid for direction. As soon as the Chinook pilots saw the gun locations, they placed the A-22 cargo nets with the ammunition just to the side of the guns. I functioned as the FDO for the left platoon, and Lt. Harris served as the FDO for the right platoon. The guns were much closer to each other than normal.

Upon landing, the CFB said he needed a direction. Lt. Harris yelled to me, "Captain, where are we? What are the coordinates?"

I replied, "I don't really know. I was hoping you knew."

Harris said everything looked the same. He had lost the capability of maintaining our location about 10 minutes after we lifted off Sandra. Unfortunately, that happened to me as well. I thought

I had a decent orientation to our new location and provided those coordinates to Lt. Harris. I had been told that most of the lucrative targets would probably be north. I told the CFB to point the tubes north and lay the battery on 6400 mils. We decided to fire the first round center of sector and cross our fingers.

We would have preferred to maintain a low profile until we began firing. However, within minutes of landing on the ridge, it seemed that the sky was full of aircraft above and near our position. Two L-19 Birddogs identified themselves as our air observers. Four or more Hueys were thundering around overhead. I later learned that our battalion commander, Lt. Col. Majikas, was in one of the aircraft. In another was Col. Putnam, the 1st Cavalry Division Artillery commander. A third air observer was in one of the helicopters.

We started receiving fire missions faster than we could compute and fire them. Many targets were preplanned based on various intelligence sources. Targets were identified as troop concentrations, equipment in the open and equipment in storage areas, and parked vehicles in the open. Our first observer correction was left 1,000 meters. *Uh-oh!* After that correction, we knew our location, and all fire missions went smoothly for the next one-and-a-half hours. Then, an excited air observer said for us to expend all ammunition on the next two fire missions and prepare for extraction.

It sounded normal to us… until Lt. Col. Majikas came on the fire net and said to "CSMO (close station march order) with all haste." The bad guys were climbing the mountain toward our position.

We were ready for extraction in record time, even before the Chinooks arrived for us. We were happy to be back on LZ Sandra.

The next day, Col. Putnam arrived on Sandra to discuss Alpha Battery's "first artillery raid." I reported to him. We sat on our steel pots (helmets) some distance from the gun line and FDC. I remember his first comment to me: "Did your battery have fun yesterday, Captain?"

We then discussed the pros and cons of our artillery raid mission for about 30 minutes. Col. Putnam complimented Alpha Battery for doing a great job of shooting and following instructions for a rapid extraction. Later, I was told that the person most worried and excited about getting us off the ridge and back to Sandra was Lt. Col. Majikas. We went on a second artillery raid in July. After that raid, the infantry colonel in charge of the 3rd Brigade forward tactical operations center (TOC) on Sandra told Majikas that he did not want any of the Alpha Battery guns to leave Sandra until his TOC left. I took that to mean that he relied on the responsive, accurate, and timely artillery fires we provided him. On reflection, perhaps he disliked the six or seven Chinooks blowing down his TOC tent every time we lifted off the tiny LZ.

Life on our small mountain top should have been boring. For some of my soldiers, I have no doubt it was. There weren't any nearby roads coming towards or coming up the mountain to our position. The part of the world within our sight was still pretty much as it had been since creation. It was accessible only by helicopter or, of course, climbing.

We soon settled into a daily routine, knowing that we were told to prepare for a stay of several weeks to a month; at the same time, I was told almost on a weekly basis that we should remain prepared to depart Sandra on less than 24-hour's notice. These instructions were passed to young American men between 18 and 22 years old. It is not in the American psyche to sit around with nothing to do in between fire missions, and sometimes fire missions occurred once or twice each hour. Other times, it could be hours between fire missions.

The six howitzer sections, fire direction section, one cook, one communications soldier, CFB, and three officers comprised Alpha Battery stationed on LZ Sandra. In total, there were 66 of us on

LZ Sandra each day. That left approximately 37 of the battery's personnel remaining on LZ English. They were the first sergeant, mess cooks, commo, maintenance, and ammunition sections. From LZ English, which was on the Bong Son plains (flat rice paddies), these sections supported the battery on LZ Sandra. Their jobs were more difficult than ours.

The resupply of 105-mm ammunition delivered by Ch-47 Chinooks carrying the ammo in an A-22 cargo net slung under the helicopter was a daily occurrence. Water blivits and field rations (C-rations) were delivered several times a week, usually on an as-needed basis. Yes, our only food was C-rations except on Fridays.

Hot food was delivered to us Fridays via Huey helicopter if the aircraft was not committed in battle, on another mission, or during heavy rains. The food was delivered in mermite containers and was always the same menu: liver, spinach, and ice cream. Well, there was probably another vegetable included. But I distinctly remember these three items, each in a separate container inside the mermite container. After bouncing around in the Huey, at least two of the foods found their way into all three containers. At first, everyone was unhappy with this. It did not take more than a few weeks before we were so hungry for real food, we did not care how mixed up the foods were. It became something we looked forward to every Friday.

These young American artillerymen were hard-pressed to remain idle for long periods. They asked for the ammunition to be transported in the two round wooden boxes rather than being removed from the boxes and delivered in their fiber containers. During lulls in firing, they reinforced their gun positions, particularly where their ammo was stored.

It was a standing joke that if someone wanted a hot meal, they simply tossed their choice of C-rations for that meal in a garbage can of boiling water for an instant hot meal. With a wonderful hot meal of C-rations, they still had to sit on the ground or a steel pot to eat it. A suggestion was made one day to create a makeshift mess hall. I said that seemed to be a great idea, but it was much like pie in the sky. Two days later, much to my surprise and amazement, construction began on what became a decent size mess hall. I did not stop the construction. The troops ate meals there, played cards, and used it as a hangout.

We even played horseshoes on LZ Sandra. OK, maybe not exactly the horseshoes you think. The troops called it "mini horseshoes," and the pieces came from the fuse end of the 105-mm projectiles after removing the rounds from the ammo boxes. The pins came from the box that held the rounds together in the box.

Being on that small high mountain knoll must have been an easy location for all low-flying aircraft to see us. Huey and Chinook pilots frequently made comments, by radio, to our FDC as they flew near us. On a couple of occasions, upon completion of bombing raids on targets near LZ Sandra, U.S. Air Force tactical aircraft slowed down when overhead and waved their wings at us. It was quite a sight. It made us proud. They could see my cannoneers returning their "wave" and jumping for joy.

In a war, and especially in an artillery battery, you are on duty and prepared to conduct fire missions 24 hours a day, 7 days a week. The XO and CFB took turns sleeping and supervising the guns. The highest-ranking enlisted man in the fire direction center was a Specialist 4 with less than two years in the Army. The FDO did not have someone to spell him for sleep or when otherwise needed. I was in and out of FDC frequently during each day to observe and help the FDO when needed. Usually, around dusk each evening, I observed the incoming defensive concentration coordinates being plotted, computed, and sometimes fired for the infantry we were supporting. After that, I took about a three- or four-hour nap. During my nap time, the H and I (Harassing and Interdiction) fire coordinates were received and plotted for firing on a predetermined time schedule throughout the late night and early morning.

I functioned as the FDO daily from 0200 hours to 0800 hours, or until the LZ artillery preparation was completed and the infantry unit had occupied the new unsecured LZ. I enjoyed this time. It was both challenging and fun. This allowed the FDO to get a decent night's sleep. I even got a few more hours of sleep later in the morning if the fire missions were not too frequent.

In late August, United States Army Vietnam (USARV) decided to give the battalion an inspector general (IG) inspection. I could not believe that was going to happen. Not all of the battery's equipment had been moved forward from Qui Nhon in October 1966. The new battalion commander, Lt. Col. Philo A. Hutcheson, ordered all battery commanders to inspect their equipment in Qui Nhon. With 1stSgt Russell and several soldiers and trucks, we traveled to Qui Nhon only to find everything in our two Conex containers were moldy and of no use or value. The contents were taken to a local dump. The IG inspection did not disrupt our support missions. And I had a chance to eat two good meals before returning to LZ Sandra.

The troops did such a good job building the mess hall, they decided to build decent sleeping quarters for the three officers. It was rare that more than one officer was asleep at any one time. The really nice sleeping quarters they built had only two bunks but included a wooden stand outside the door where we could fill our steel pot with water, wash up, and shave. The arrangement was much better than how we did these functions previously. It was always our job to take care of our troops. In this case, it was our troops taking care of us.

Their construction efforts did not end there. Soon, an open-air shower appeared in the middle of the howitzer firing positions, a location that actually made sense. If you are taking a shower and the radios blare "Fire Mission," you get to your gun section with all haste. With or without clothes!

LZ Sandra's single shower for 66 artillerymen located in the howitzers' position area, September 1967. Water was a scarce commodity on the LZ. Pictured here is Capt. Collier enjoying an afternoon shower. Photo provided to Capt. Collier by the Alpha Battery XO, 1st Lt. Dan Benton. Photo provided by Col. Bill Collier.

The shower canvas bag held less than two gallons of water, if I remember correctly. Two people would take a shower before the bag needed to be refilled. So, you got wet quickly, turned the shower nozzle off, soaped down, turned the shower nozzle on, and rinsed very quickly before turning the shower nozzle off again. If you used more than your share of the water, there was a penalty that will not be discussed here.

LZ Sandra soon became known as a location that had a continuing target-rich environment. There were two times when 155 mm howitzers were collocated with my battery to attack targets at ranges greater than we could engage. These 155 mm batteries would depart after a week or so when the need for them ceased. I recall that one of the batteries was Alpha Battery, 1st Battalion, 30th Artillery. The battery commander was Capt. McNulty.

I departed LZ Sandra on the morning of October 5, 1967. As a Chinook helicopter was depositing some 105 mm ammo, I asked

LZ Sandra: August 1967. Officers' sleeping quarters under construction just outside the Fire Direction Center. Construction crew: our cannoneers! Photo by Col. Bill Collier.

the pilot for a ride to LZ English. He said, "OK," sat down, lowered his rear ramp, and I happily climbed aboard. I told him I was rotating home today. He took the helicopter on a "nap of the earth" ride back to LZ English, which scared me nearly to death. When I asked why he did that, he said he wanted to get me to LZ English without anyone shooting at us. I told him I would have preferred taking my chances at 2,000 feet. He smiled and saluted. I made it to Camp Alpha on Bien Hoa Air Base near Saigon and departed Vietnam on or about October 10.

In 2012, I learned that Alpha Battery came off LZ Sandra approximately a week after I left LZ Sandra. The battery was relocated to LZ Tom near the town of Tam Quan on the Bong Son coastal plain.

I also learned why LZ Sandra was such a target-rich environment. It seems that the 22nd NVA Regiment of the 3rd NVA Division had been traveling the An Loa Valley's floor for months. Going eastward from the Central Highlands to the Bong Son Plains, they had to pass by or around the mountain with LZ Sandra on top. From time to time, elements of this unit would be spotted and attacked either by artillery or infantry. On December 6, 1967, they were spotted and engaged near the town of Tan Quan. A ferocious battle ensued that lasted until December 20.

Alpha Battery, 7th Battalion, 13th Artillery supported the 1st Cavalry Division and the 1st Battalion, 150th Mechanized, 50th Infantry extremely well during this battle. I was pleased and proud to learn of their performance.

CHAPTER FIVE
RETURN TO VIETNAM

IN 1967, THE NUMBER OF YOUNG combat-experienced artillery battery commanders was relatively low but rapidly increasing as additional U.S. Army divisions continued to be inserted into South Vietnam. The policy was for artillery captains to command batteries for no more than six months. In my case, my battalion commander, Lt. Col. Majikas, changed command at my six-month date in early August 1967. The incoming battalion commander, Lt. Col. Hutcheson, asked me to remain as Alpha Battery's commander for a few weeks longer until he could decide who would replace me. I guess he had difficulty with decision-making, as I remained on as BC until rotating back to the U.S. on October 10. I served eight months and some days as a firing battery commander in Vietnam.

All things considered, it was not a surprise that I was reassigned to the Field Artillery School at Ft. Sill, OK. In fact, I expected and hoped for such an assignment. My experiences in Vietnam were later integrated into lesson plans subsequently taught to students of artillery.

Life was good again. In March of 1970, I received orders for Germany. That would be fine with me, as long as the Army did not change its mind again, as it had done in 1966.

By 1970, many of my fellow officers were being reassigned to Vietnam for a second tour of duty. The normal tour length in Germany was three years. It would not be desirable to go to

Germany for a three-year tour and then get orders for a second tour in Vietnam before my Germany tour was completed. I did not want that to happen to my family or me.

I "took the bull by the horns," as the saying goes, and called the Military Personnel Center in Alexandria, VA, from whence all major reassignment orders originate. I explained that if I were to be reassigned for a second tour in Vietnam, then I preferred to do it at that time, and after that tour, be assigned to Germany. The assignment officer was very nice and said things I enjoyed hearing. He may have been a lieutenant colonel who, when answering the telephone, said, "This is Colonel So-and-So." We called them "telephone colonels." Later, as a lieutenant colonel, I was a telephone colonel until a real colonel told me that was not ethical.

But, back to the conversation. He stated that those returning to Vietnam were going on their second short tour, meaning they were unaccompanied by family members. I had already been to Korea and Vietnam for my two short tours and was not eligible for a third short tour unless I volunteered. As I was not volunteering, I should proceed on to Germany and enjoy my three years there.

Great. Just the information I wanted to hear.

My family and I arrived in Germany in June 1970 to find that the 2nd Battalion, 92nd Artillery Battalion, had traveled to Grafenwoehr the day before for a 35-day training period. The next day, an open-air jeep arrived to take me to Grafenwoehr, some 200 miles from Giessen, Germany, to join this eight-inch short tube nuclear-capable battalion. I had been assigned as the S-3 operations officer. Fortunately, the battalion commander's wife was a wonderful lady and helped my family get settled during my absence.

Germany was a great assignment. We were enjoying the culture, the people, and learning to speak German. The beer was especially good. The Germans seemed to welcome us everywhere we went. The English language was required for the first 10 years of schooling in Germany. After we tried to make ourselves understood in German, they would then switch to English for our comfort and greater understanding. However, if we didn't try to speak German, most people would not let us know they spoke English.

Interesting.

Our ongoing war in Vietnam had depleted many resources otherwise devoted to our forces in Europe, including personnel. For example, the battalion sergeant major's position was filled by a former high school teacher drafted into the Army who was now a Specialist 4. His duties were mostly administrative, of course. The gun chiefs were E-5s rather than E-6s. Most positions were filled by ranks lower than authorized. The personnel situation at that time was worrisome.

After I had been with the battalion for a year, the battalion executive officer completed his three-year tour and returned to the U.S. I was offered the XO position and accepted it. That position primarily involved monitoring all levels of battalion maintenance. Track vehicular maintenance was a very real problem during this time. I took advantage of an opportunity to attend a three-week officers maintenance course offered in Murnau, Germany, from late September to October 1971.

While attending this maintenance course, I received orders for a second tour in Vietnam.

Really? This can't be happening. Unbelievable. This is déjà vu all over again!

I promptly called PERSCOM (Personnel Command), located outside of Heidelberg. After my detailed explanation of my conversation with MILPERCEN a year or so earlier, in my calmest voice, his response was disappointing. It was more or less: "OK, I hear you, so what? That is the way the cookie crumbles. You got orders. You are going back to Vietnam. You are leaving Germany in December 1971." Then this PERSCOM lieutenant colonel heard the same explanation of my conversation with the MILPERCEN colonel, in an entirely different tone of voice, loud enough for the dead to hear. I thought perhaps he had not clearly heard my first explanation. He said he heard both explanations, but he still did not care.

"You are still going back to Vietnam," he said.

My family and I departed Germany on December 23, arriving at my wife's home on Christmas Day. Santa Claus got lost in the move, but he found us the next day, which quickly restored my children's belief in him.

After short visits with both sides of our family, my family and I arrived in Arlington, VA, in early January 1972, where I reported for training in the Military District Senior Advisors Course, Foreign Service Institute, at the U.S. Department of State. We were fortunate to find a suitable apartment within a mile of the Foreign Service Institute. It was within walking distance for me, and the children were satisfactorily enrolled in school. So, the family settled down for five months of a new adventure.

The Foreign Service Institute was well organized and prepared for our class. As best as I can recall, there were 34 officers, all majors, with one exception, a lieutenant colonel. They provided us with several statistics and what could be considered warnings. For example, my class would be the last to receive this training, and in consideration of the rigorous drawdown of American combat units in Vietnam during the previous two years, casualties within the class could be somewhat higher than those of previous classes. Such words of comfort and reassurance served to make us so pleased that we had been selected for this class.

The primary objective of the training we were about to undertake was for each student to attain a reasonable, albeit minimal, level of proficiency in the Vietnamese language. Vietnamese is a tonal language where one word can have five tones, each with a different meaning. This posed problems for a person like me, raised in the southern part of the United States. I struggled with learning Vietnamese for the first two months until, suddenly, the light bulb seemed to glow a little brighter.

It never really got *easy* for me, though. The Vietnamese instructors were patient. Upon graduation, I believed I would never progress beyond the very basics, even when I got to Vietnam. Amazingly, after several months of living with the Vietnamese, I could sometimes have a limited conversations with the locals. My assigned interpreter helped me through questionable spots during selected conversations. It was actually fun. Often, the villagers would start laughing, which was my clue that I had used an incorrect tone. It was easy to see that they appreciated that I was trying to speak their language. That alone was encouraging to me.

In addition to language instruction, we received a healthy dose of cultural training. Neither the State Department nor MILPERCEN knew which advisory team any of us would be assigned to. Therefore, we were taught the geography of South Vietnam, selected cultural aspects, and influential historical events that could have an impact on the area's current attitudes. This training proved to be very beneficial.

Guest speakers provided interesting and informative presentations almost weekly. These speakers included general officers, several ambassadors who were probably home for retraining or reassignment, and other well-placed people in the State Department.

By the time our training concluded in May, most of us felt comfortable about our pending assignment to Vietnam. We were given a fancy graduation ceremony. We believed that we were better prepared for our duty in Vietnam this time.

I was later told that numerous members of this class were awarded the Purple Heart. The last soldier to die in the Vietnam war was an MACV team advisor and allegedly a member of this class. This class was in Vietnam when the *Agreement on Ending the War and Restoring Peace in Vietnam* was signed on January 27, 1973. A number of us also served on the *Four Party Joint Military Commission,* which supervised the return of our captured military personnel, from January 29-March 29, 1973. This assignment and experience will be discussed in a later chapter.

DEPARTMENT OF STATE

FOREIGN SERVICE INSTITUTE

VIET-NAM TRAINING CENTER

THIS CERTIFICATE IS AWARDED TO

Major William P. Collier, Jr.

IN RECOGNITION OF SATISFACTORY COMPLETION OF THE TRAINING PROGRAM

FOR CIVIL OPERATIONS AND RURAL DEVELOPMENT SUPPORT, VIET-NAM

JANUARY 17 – MAY 19, 1972

Barbara W. Morlet
ADMISSIONS OFFICER

Raymond G Jones
COORDINATOR

Foreign Service Institute Certificate

CHAPTER SIX
MO DUC DISTRICT,
QUANG NGAI PROVINCE

I N 1972, QUANG Ngai Province was a beautiful land politically divided into 10 geographical districts with an approximate population of 750,000. Six districts abundant with rice paddies were located in the lowlands: Duc Pho, Mo Duc, Tu Nghia, Nghia Hanh, Son Tinh, and Binh Son. The remaining four were in the western mountainous areas: Ba To, Minh Long, Son Ha, and Tra Bong. These districts had a total of 112 villages and 339 hamlets. A Vietnamese province is analogous to states in the United States; districts are like counties, villages are like small cities, and hamlets are comparable to subdivisions in a city. These comparisons are solely my definitions, provided for your ease.

Much of the culture and daily life of the local Vietnamese people I encountered had deep roots in their history, which still impacted them as if unchanged throughout the years. Some of the outcomes during the September 16-18, 1972, attempt by the combined forces of the Viet Cong and the North Vietnam Army (NVA) to overrun the Mo Duc district can be directly related to events and personalities in their recent 100-year history, most notably from colonization by the French in 1886, up to and including the American involvement in South Vietnam beginning in 1959.

Unsuccessful challenges to French control by the Vietnamese over the years eroded French control during the 1930s. During World War II, a nationalistic front organization called the League for the Independence of Vietnam, later called the Viet Minh, gained strength throughout Vietnam under the leadership of Ho Chi Minh. Their rise in popularity was accelerated by the unwelcome presence of a small Japanese force headquartered in Saigon, along with the continuing presence of the French colonial government. After V-J Day in 1945, the Viet Minh became the de facto government and maintained their control throughout the countryside during the nine-year struggle against the French. Quang Ngai province became the major Viet Minh base of operations in central Vietnam.

Following the defeat of the French at Bien Dien Phu in 1954 and the Geneva Agreement that same year, Vietnam was divided into North Vietnam and South Vietnam. Viet Minh from many areas in the south gathered in Quang Ngai province before sailing to North Vietnam. The national elections stipulated and agreed to in the Geneva Agreement did not occur. Thereafter, North Vietnam was soon considered a communist regime.

The Viet Minh, now called the Viet Cong (Vietnamese Communist) or VC for short, began infiltrating south into the mountains of Quang Ngai province. As their strength and numbers increased, military raids into the districts of the provinces occurred. After the government of President Ngo Dinh Diem collapsed in 1963, the Viet Cong were able to gain control of most of the mountainous areas and also of large areas of the lowlands, except for the district towns.

The Government of Vietnam (GVN) had fought to regain the area under Viet Cong control. Their progress was slow until the TET Offensive in 1968. Communist forces had expected a popular uprising. This did not occur, and, subsequently, the communist forces were soundly defeated and withdrew. However, Quang Ngai province continued to be a hotbed for communist support, which slowed the retaking of land from the Viet Cong.

MO DUC DISTRICT

The entire district itself was essentially rural. Electricity throughout Mo Duc was non-existent. The district of Mo Duc had seven villages and numerous hamlets with a population of approximately 80,000 in 1972. A refugee camp of 10,000 to 30,000 people was located adjacent to the district headquarters near the hamlet of Mo Duc. The population of this refugee camp brought the total Mo Duc district population to something approaching 110,000. The refugee population had more than doubled during the spring and summer of 1972 as a result of the offensive initiated by the VC and NVA in April 1972.

A major offensive by the VC and the NVA in April 1972 forced the GVN to relinquish the areas they had newly acquired over the previous two years, especially in eastern Binh Son, Son Tinh, Mo Duc, and southern Duc Pho. Apparently, their successes gave them the confidence to conduct another major offensive five months later, in September 1972.

Mo Duc had traditionally been one of the most difficult and dangerous districts in Vietnam because of a deep-rooted Viet Cong infrastructure dating to the Viet Minh control of Mo Duc district from 1945 to 1954. In Mo Duc, it was believed that nearly every citizen and family was, in some way, linked to the VC.

MO DUC DISTRICT HEADQUARTERS

The Mo Duc district headquarters was not much to write home about. The headquarters was probably built or greatly improved by the French during their occupation in earlier decades. The entire compound was encircled with several rows of concertina wire on the outside, with approximately 20 yards of open area before a second ring of double concertina also encircled the compound. In between the two rows of double concertina, numerous claymore anti-personnel mines were emplaced. The compound also had several firing ports protected by overhead concrete ceilings and concrete walls. These firing ports were located on the perimeter inside the concertina wire to the north and south. There were also two jeeps with .50 caliber machine guns mounted on them and an open vehicle parking area. This area did not have any protective cover or concealment. The entire district headquarters compound was not quite as large as an American football field.

Rice paddies and small hamlets were on the northeast and southeast sides of MSR-1 (Main Supply Route or Highway 1) facing the district headquarters. There was a hamlet on the northwestern side and a refugee camp on the western side. The population of the refugee camp had recently increased so much that the eastern edge, which included a schoolhouse, was 30 to 50 meters from the northwestern perimeter of the district headquarters. Rice paddies occupied most of the land both north and south of the district headquarters compound.

Upon my arrival for duty in June 1972, the district operations officer told me that the refugee camp population had grown to 10,000 to 12,000 over the past several years. However, the situation in the western mountainous areas, especially since April of 1972, had caused a significant increase in the camp's population. By September, the camp's population was estimated to be as high as 25,000, maybe more. When viewed from the air, it was difficult to tell where the local village and hamlets stopped and the refugee camp began. On the ground, the distinction was quite obvious due to the inferior living conditions in the refugee camp and the rank smells.

From Highway 1 westward, a two-lane dirt road led to the district headquarters' only gate, which was approximately 100 meters with a few structures on the south side part of the way. The last 30 to 40 meters of the road was across an open area. Just outside the gate and slightly north was a small helipad. Rice paddies were on the north side.

Inside the district compound, the western and northern perimeters had solid one-story typical Vietnamese buildings with orange-colored clay shingled roofs. On the southern end of the western perimeter was a building that housed troops. The western perimeter also contained buildings housing the military dispensary, jail, the

TOC, and sundry offices. The northwestern perimeter had an 81mm mortar position with a sufficient stockpile of mortar rounds and a sleeping area for two mortarmen. Also on the northwestern perimeter were buildings for the district chief and those who supported him.

MACV DISTRICT ADVISOR
TEAM 17 ACCOMMODATIONS

The MACV District Advisor Team 17 building and separate team sleeping quarters/bunker were located in the north-central part of the northern perimeter. The team house was nondescript and similar to most of the buildings in the compound. This team building housed an office with radios, a small sitting and reading room, a dining room, a kitchen, and a bathroom with a toilet and shower. Team members from previous years had built the team's separate but adjacent sleeping quarters. This structure appeared to be a stronger building than all the others. The roof had a layer of sandbags for added protection. None of these accommodations were fancy, but it was good living compared to my accommodations as an artillery Battery Commander with the 1st Air Cavalry in 1967.

In the center of the compound was a flagpole where the flag of the Republic of Vietnam was ceremoniously raised and lowered each day. If we walked directly south some 20 meters out our team house front door, we would be at the flagstaff.

OBSERVATION TOWER

Adjacent and west of our team house was a tall, sturdy concrete observation tower also built by the French. This tower was approximately 30 to 40 feet tall. It was the first thing one could see from several miles away when approaching Mo Duc headquarters. The entrance was through a semi-secluded area, which meant that access was limited to a very few. Stairs led from the ground floor to the two observation levels. Observation was excellent from the third level, with firing ports on both the second and third levels, as well as wider open windows on the third level. Two-foot vertical slits on all four sides easily allowed for 360-degree observation.

During my first week, I took a tour of the tower, but I was never invited back for a second visit. During my one-time visit to the tower, I was able to see the South China Sea to the east and the densely covered mountains to the west. Basically, the eastern and central land of Mo Duc district was flat with an abundance of rice paddies. Patches of jungle existed throughout with banana trees. These areas of jungle were also great areas to conceal many types of activities.

When I inquired as to the activity of people in the tower, the district chief simply shrugged it off by saying it was a rest-and-recreation area for some of his officers. As a trained field artillery forward observer, it was obvious that this tower was extremely significant for its military value. I'm quite sure that was the reason it was built in the first place. I was puzzled that the district made little use of it. Or did they?

Mo Duc district compound: French-built observation tower looking north, June 1972. Photo by Col. Bill Collier.

Aerial view of the Mo Duc district headquarters, the adjacent refugee camp, the hamlets of Mo Duc and Dong Cat, and LZ Dragon (Nui Khoang), August 1972. Photo by Col. Bill Collier.

The Mo Duc district headquarters is the approximate square set of buildings near the middle of the picture, August 1972. The refugee camp structures are those rectangular buildings not situated among palm trees. Other structures are the hamlets surrounding the district headquarters. Photo by Col. Bill Collier.

An 81-mm mortar pit inside the northwest side of Mo Duc district headquarters, September 1972. Photo by Col. Bill Collier.

CHAPTER SEVEN
THE GENERAL'S VISIT

T HE AMERICAN DRAWDOWN of U.S. combat forces was essentially completed by the summer of 1972. The 7th Battalion, 13th Artillery I served in from 1966-1967, supporting the 1st Cavalry Division, was deactivated in 1970. The 1st Cavalry Division had been relocated to Fort Hood, TX. Over the next two years, most of the separate American battalions, separate brigades, full divisions, and combat and logistical support units were also deactivated or relocated to the U.S. By August 1972, U.S. Army units in the field were primarily small American district and province-level advisory teams and advisors with several Army of the Republic of Vietnam (ARVN) divisions and Ranger units throughout South Vietnam to train and mentor their ARVN forces.

The only military units in Quang Ngai province were the Vietnamese Territorial Forces. I equated them to our National Guard. The majority of these troops were from local villages and hamlets, with some ARVN soldiers scattered throughout their ranks. They were sometimes affectionately called "Rough Puffs." These forces were organized as Regional Forces (RF) and Popular Forces (PF). The PF was organized as platoons with soldiers recruited from the same area the platoon was assigned. Their mission was to provide security for their hamlet. Mo Duc had 54 PF platoons. The RF had infantry companies that seemed somewhat better trained. Their soldiers could be from the local village as well as other villages in the district. The RF operated throughout the district to provide security for the villages. Mo Duc had seven RF companies.

In March 1972, allegedly 14 North Vietnamese Army (NVA) divisions crossed into South Vietnam. This action became known as the "Spring" or "Easter" Offensive. Initially, we thought their units only attacked throughout the province of Quang Tri. Soon we learned that many of their units also traveled through Laos and Cambodia, ostensibly on the Ho Chi Minh trail with predetermined military objectives in South Vietnam all along the length of South Vietnam's western border. Their offensive was designed to topple the South Vietnamese government or, at the very least, to strengthen their position at the ongoing peace negotiation talks in Paris.

By the time I had been the District Senior Advisor (DSA) in Mo Duc for three months, I had been on many boring and seemingly useless "walks in the sun" types of operations, approximately 12 small firefights, and one scary-as-hell ambush. Capt. Nguyen, the operations officer, told me that since my arrival, Viet Cong (VC) activity in Mo Duc and throughout Quang Ngai had been somewhat decreasing from what they had previously experienced. He did not know why. That comment did not have much meaning to me. I had no way to compare "decreasing activity when compared to former activity."

For the previous month or so, the Mo Duc District Operations Center had been receiving spot reports about the presence of NVA soldiers and units moving into and through various areas of Quang Ngai province's western districts. Initially, these reports were not cause for concern. Too often during those times, reports were inaccurate, misinterpreted, or even intentionally entered into the intelligence gathering community for various and obvious reasons.

UNHEEDED WARNINGS

However, beginning in late August 1972 and continuing in early September, the reports allegedly contained information about NVA soldiers close to (and sometimes in) the western areas of Mo Duc district. That is when Capt. Nguyen began drawing my attention to these reports. Usually, I was not apprised of routine combat-related radio or other communication traffic.

Capt. Nguyen seemed quite fixated on these reports. I asked if he had made the district chief aware of the reports, as well as his personal concern. He said he had spoken up but that the district chief was not alarmed and quickly dismissed the authenticity of these incoming reports.

Until this point, my relationship with ARVN District Chief Lt. Col. Thanh, my counterpart and the individual I was supposed to be advising, was not as cordial, open, and receptive as I had hoped. Perhaps this was an opportunity to improve my relationship with him.

Thanh, a lieutenant colonel in the Army of the Republic of Vietnam at the time, had been a member of the Viet Minh, supported by the communists in their fight against the French during the late 1940s until the French were defeated in 1954. To some of his staff and civilian visitors, he seemed to be a celebrity.

I followed the protocol he had established for daily appointments. It took the better part of a day to get on his calendar. I raised the issue of the recurring reports of NVA units in and around the western mountainous areas of Mo Duc. He immediately responded in a matter-of-fact manner that he was aware of these reports. In fact, he said he had been personally involved in the investigation and could find no evidence to substantiate the reports. I left our meeting with doubts about the reports. And I did *not* believe I succeeded in improving my relationship with my counterpart.

Capt. Nguyen was somewhat smaller in stature than most of the Vietnamese in Mo Duc. He seemed to be highly intelligent, efficient, and dedicated to his job as the district operations officer. He usually went on most operations. Overall, I was impressed with him as an officer and as an individual. It seemed that he placed more credence on the reports of enemy presence than did the district chief. What should I do?

I made the decision to continue forwarding the content of these reports up my American chain of command during the first week of September. Soon, my boss Col. Truman Bowman asked me to come to Quang Ngai City to discuss the reports. I must have sufficiently convinced him that the reports and Capt. Nguyen's analysis had merit. The reports were thereafter forwarded up his chain of command. Col. Bowman discussed the reports with his province chief, who later told Col. Bowman that the district chief had looked into the matter and could not substantiate the reports. Even so, Col. Bowman supported me and forwarded my daily reports.

THE GENERAL'S VISIT

On September 15, 1972, I was notified that a visitor from the Military Advisory Command Vietnam (MACV) in Saigon was enroute to visit me. I wondered if this was a routine visit for MACV to monitor their teams in the districts and provinces… Or was it to discuss my reports of NVA sightings in Mo Duc?

I suspected the latter.

The effects of an offshore typhoon were still very much present on September 15 as the visitor made his way. Low clouds and light-to-medium rain seemed to hamper movement on the ground. I had not seen nor heard anything in the air for two days. I thought that my approaching visitor might be "weathered out," as was the saying in those days.

My visitor from Saigon arrived by Huey helicopter in the afternoon. His helicopter sat down on the small helipad immediately outside of the Mo Duc district headquarters, where I greeted him. Much to my surprise, he was an American brigadier general. I quickly realized from the exchange of salutes that our chemistry was not good. He gave the impression that his visit was either not necessary or a nuisance to him at the very least. Perhaps he was not happy about flying in this weather.

When he asked where we could talk, I suggested my small team office. He went straight to the purpose of his visit. He wanted an explanation concerning the content of the American advisor reports and the absence of the same vital information in the ARVN reporting channels.

The general's mission was to discuss my almost daily reports of NVA sightings in western Mo Duc districts. He informed me that he had read my reports and had not only discussed them with my chain of command, but also with our host country members. No one could or would agree with any of the information in my reports. He said that either I needed to have positive proof validating my reports or that I was to stop forwarding such unsubstantiated information, which upset both our allies and the American chain of command.

My only defense was to reiterate my belief in the professionalism of Capt. Nguyen. The captain told me that several PF platoons in different western locations had provided the information, so I continued to believe the reports were accurate.

I suggested that the general speak directly to Nguyen. He flatly stated that would not be necessary, nor did he want to talk with the district chief. The general looked me in the eye and got too close for my comfort. He said, "Major, I think you are too nervous working out here in the boonies. For your own good, I recommend you go to Vung Tau for a week of in-country rest and recuperation to see if that will do you any good."

I knew that Vung Tau was a beautiful beach city that Americans and our allies went to for relaxation during the war. Frankly, I felt his recommendation was an insult and an embarrassment to me.

Our meeting wrapped up around 1700 hours on September 15, 1972. I asked the general to spend the night with us, perhaps ride through the refugee camp and watch the District Operations Center for a while during the evening. At that point, he seemed insulted and said he was leaving to return to Saigon. I knew he would not stay. I even had my fingers crossed, hoping he would not stay the night. The weather was not good, with standing water in most places where we walked. To be truthful, our accommodations were still quite spartan, especially compared to what the general was provided in Saigon.

As I watched his Huey depart, I began to doubt my ability to determine reality from all the confusing information made available to me.

Maybe the general was right. He is a general officer, after all. Generals were supposed to be squared away. Maybe I should go to Vung Tau.

I decided to sleep on that thought.

TYPHOON FLOSSIE

Many roads were now impassable due to the rains, and rice paddies, hamlets, and villages were somewhat flooded. A small waterway, the Thoa River which flowed from the northwest to the southwest, had overflowed its banks, coupled with a strong current. About two miles north of Mo Duc, the river divided into several small tributaries, or what Americans considered to be streams or creeks. They, too, were greatly swollen. The weather was windy with low, thick clouds and intermittent rain showers.

To avoid the typhoon, the U.S. Navy had sailed further out into the South China Sea. Most of the remaining U.S. Air Force (USAF) planes had relocated to Ubon, Thailand. The movement to Thailand included most of the USAF planes based in Da Nang. This also included all land-based rescue helicopters. None of these units and their equipment had yet returned.

The team medic, Staff Sgt. "Doc" Bassinet, had driven in the morning to the American Province Advisor Team 17 headquarters in Quang Ngai City to pick up our mail, grab a movie for us to watch, and procure anything else that would make life a little more comfortable for the team members. After 1700 hours, as my visiting general was departing, Bassinet radioed me to say he was on the way back and was already in the southern part of Tu Nghia district. The cloud cover was getting lower and thicker, and he was returning a bit later than usual. I was concerned about the slower movement on partially muddy roads, the impending nightfall, and the reports of NVA in the northern part of Mo Duc. Consequently, I told Bassinet to return to the province headquarters, spend the night, and return to Mo Duc in the morning.

DISTRICT ADVISOR TEAM 17

In addition to the three Americans, I had four Vietnamese soldiers assigned to my team. I never had any reason to doubt their loyalty to my team or any shortcomings in their performance. In my opinion, all four were completely trustworthy.

Sergeant First Class (SFC) Long was better educated than most Vietnamese I dealt with throughout the district. He was an ARVN soldier assigned as an interpreter to support the American advisor team in Mo Duc. He was married with two small children, and I would guess him to be in his late 20s. They lived in Dong Cat hamlet in a typical small straw-thatched structure. In late July, he took me to his home for brief introductions to his family. SFC Long usually spent the late evenings and nights with his family in their hamlet home. His ability to speak and write English was superior. On days when we did not leave the compound, he would study English and talk with team members about the U.S. After seven years with Americans each day, he spoke English with just a small hint of an accent. His pet peeve was that, through his years with the Americans, some of them referred to the Vietnamese as "the little people."

Then there was Sandy, who joined our team in August. He, too, was an ARVN soldier assigned as an interpreter and was better educated than most. He wanted an American name and thus took the name of Sandy when he arrived. I cannot remember his Vietnamese name. Sandy was a sergeant, probably E-5 equivalent, and was recently married. He and his wife were not from the district and had just moved to Mo Duc. He brought his dog with him. Of course, the dog quickly became "our team dog." The dog stayed with the team as Sandy feared he might become some family's meal in rural Mo Duc. I never had the opportunity to meet his wife. Sandy's English was not as capable as SFC Long's. Staff Sgt. Jackson had not attended Vietnamese language training in the U.S. and wanted Sandy with him most of the time.

Sammy was a local man in his 40s. He rarely wore any type of shoes, and his feet looked like worn leather. Sammy always had a smile on his face. As a PF platoon soldier, he was assigned as a team bodyguard, yet he actually functioned as our handyman. He could repair just about anything we had and was constantly looking for things to do to help the team's physical environment. He had two daughters. One daughter prepared our evening meal most, but not all, evenings, and the other washed our clothes three times each week. I hasten to add that teaching the daughter who made our meals to cook was a never-ending and mostly unsuccessful effort.

Wino was a local man in his late 40s or early 50s. He, too, was a PF platoon member assigned as a team bodyguard. No one knew much about Wino. You can only guess why previous advisors had named him Wino. He looked much older than his years, as if alcoholism had taken its toll. Still, not once did I smell anything on or around him that resembled alcohol. Wherever we went in the compound, I could see Wino watching one of us from a distance. He was totally reliable and spent most nights sleeping outside our team bunker door. About once every week to ten days, Wino would pass along a message to me via SFC Long that he was going to stay in the village that night. We suspected he had a girlfriend, but no one could verify that.

That evening, my District Advisor Team 17 enjoyed watching the Clint Eastwood movie *Dirty Harry*. In addition to me as the district senior advisor (DSA), Team 17 consisted of Staff Sergeant Carroll Jackson (operations advisor), "Doc" Bassinet (the medic who was in Quang Ngai City that evening), ARVN SFC Long (a very competent interpreter who had been with the team for seven-plus years), ARVN Sgt. Sandy (a second interpreter who had been with the team for only five weeks), and Sammy and Wino (two bodyguards and both PF platoon members). The team was authorized an American captain, but he transferred out in August.

That evening, September 15, 1972, was the last time this team would ever be together again.

CHAPTER EIGHT
THE BATTLE FOR MO DUC, FIRST DAY

SATURDAY, 16 SEPTEMBER 1972
APPROXIMATELY 0400 HOURS

Around 0400 hours, the Regional Force (RF) 190 Company (CO) with four Popular Force (PF) platoons came under heavy mortar and ground attack. This Observation Post (OP) is located in Thach Tru hamlet, Duc My village, located approximately five miles south of Mo Duc district headquarters.

Eventually, these units were forced off the OP, withdrawing into the village headquarters.

Emboldened by their rapid success, the North Vietnamese Army (NVA) forces pursued their planned attacks and completely captured the populated areas of Duc My village by 0930 hours with little resistance. The remaining forces of RF 190 CO were ordered to reposition in the Chau Me OP and did comply with this order.

ON OR ABOUT 0430 HOURS

The Sub-Sector (District) Operations Officer, Capt. Nguyen sent a runner to the American sleeping bunker to summon the advisor team.

The two assigned bodyguards, Sammy and Wino, usually slept outside the American advisor team bunker near the bunker entrance. Wino and Sammy stopped the runner.

The general's comments and attitude from the day before were forefront in my mind as I went to bed a few hours earlier, which should have affected my sleep. But with heavy rain falling throughout the night, I was sleeping quite peacefully on my cot when I was abruptly awakened by loud voices. The three men were noticeably upset as they tried to make me understand why the runner was there. My interpreter, Sergeant First Class (SFC) Long, was in the hamlet with his family, and the other interpreter, Sandy, was a little slow in awakening. I did not understand all the details as they were talking so fast. Their emotions clearly told me they were not there for morning coffee. I jumped up, put on my pants and boots, grabbed my weapon, and hustled to the District Tactical Operations Center (TOC).

I quickly met with Capt. Nguyen in the TOC and was briefed on what little information he knew about the Duc My village situation. He was not sure who had conducted the attack or what their intentions were, and he didn't know the significance of the attack. I suggested this could be a strong Viet Cong (VC) action designed to take advantage of the weather and probable slack security by the local RF and PF units. Nguyen said the RF190 CO commander was always reliable and would never let his soldiers be anything less than fully alert. He believed this was more than simply a VC probing action. He seemed considerably more nervous than usual. The captain was silent as he stared at the situation map as if he was trying to extract a clear interpretation to tell me of the existing danger we were facing. Sadly, he did not have much information at this point. The general's sudden visit from the afternoon before and his insinuating remarks were still reverberating in my head, so I was reluctant to offer any other comments.

I looked around for Army of the Republic of Vietnam (ARVN) District Chief, Lt. Col. Nguyen Van Thanh. He had not yet arrived in the TOC. He was probably getting dressed more completely than I had, as I was without my fatigue jacket and clad only in my green

T-shirt. Nonetheless, his leadership and instructions were sorely needed at this time.

As we were discussing the situation, we began to hear impacting mortars and rifle and machine guns firing to our west. *Could the reports of NVA presence over the last three or so weeks actually be true?*

Upon returning to our bunker, I woke Staff Sgt. Carroll Jackson and Sandy and hastily apprised them of the Duc My village situation. They, too, heard the mortar and small arms firing and were questioning who could be firing at this early hour.

Jackson was instructed to inspect the perimeter to assess how many of the District Chief's ARVN soldiers were on guard duty, determine the quantity of ammunition distributed to each defensive dugout and position along the 360-degree perimeter, and determine their general state of readiness. I finished dressing, which included everything needed for battle if it came to that. I then returned to the TOC.

0500 HOURS

The District TOC routinely maintained 24-hour communications with all seven Regional Force companies and most of the 54 Popular Force platoons. While Staff Sgt. Jackson was inspecting our perimeter, he continued hearing mortars impacting to our west. He quickly ran to the TOC to inform me. At the same time, Capt. Nguyen received news that NVA forces had launched a mortar and ground attack against the ARVN artillery battery (Battery C, 21st Artillery) on Landing Zone Dragon (American units named this LZ in the 1960s).

An artillery battery usually has six guns. The battery on LZ Dragon only had two 105mm howitzers. The LZ was located on the Nui Khoang plateau, approximately 800 meters west of the Mo Duc district headquarters. A Government of Vietnam (GVN) Sub-Sector OP was also located on the north end of the plateau, and a district OP, named the Thiet Truong OP, was 1,700 meters from them on the south end. This plateau is the highest natural terrain for observation closest to but west of the Mo Duc district headquarters. In other words, it was a key and valuable piece of terrain from a military viewpoint. It made perfect sense that any enemy force would want this piece of terrain near the outset of their attack.

The artillery commander verified that the attackers were NVA soldiers. He was surprised by the ferocity of the attack. Within 30 minutes, the artillery position had been overrun. The artillerymen managed to destroy one of the two 105mm howitzers before withdrawing into the adjoining Sub-Sector OP. I later learned that the conquering NVA soldiers were unable to effectively operate the remaining 105mm howitzer, thereby sparing the district compound in the first few critical hours of their attack. That was a blessing. The enemy forces continued their aggressive attack on this OP, which was occupied by HQ 1/30 RF CO Group, some elements of RF 183 CO, one PF platoon, and the artillery survivors.

The survivors later stated that each of the above-cited positions was attacked from the west by a heavy barrage of mortar fire and human-wave ground assaults. At 0700 hours, we learned that the Thiet Truong OP fell into enemy hands. Almost all the friendly forces were killed, with the few survivors employing escape and evasion movements as they sought refuge in various hamlets and villages.

I looked around for the district chief. Where was he? He should have been leading the defense of the district headquarters compound and ARVN forces throughout the district of Mo Duc. After all the commotion and mortars landing around us, he most certainly should have been awake and taking command of all his responsibilities. So far that morning, I had not seen nor heard from him. I asked Capt. Nguyen if someone had been to Lt. Col. Thanh's quarters. He just looked at me momentarily and, without answering, continued plotting reports of enemy actions. I was not sure how to react to his response to me. I thought it was best to say nothing. We had more serious issues to deal with at that point.

0530 HOURS

NVA mortar fire began to rain on and near the Mo Duc district headquarters. The volume of fire was heavy and continuous. The district TOC radios were now alive with frantic calls for help and intelligence reports. The radio traffic was overriding each other, making audible comprehension often impossible. We all looked at each other and, without saying a word, suddenly realized that the weeks of NVA sightings were true. The NVA forces were out in the open now and simultaneously attacking many territorial unit locations district-wide. Emotions were high. Confusion was rampant. Everyone wanted to do something, but no one knew what to do at that precise moment. You can count me as one of those who really wanted to panic. Even Capt. Nguyen looked stunned as he found a chair and sat down.

For the next few minutes, which seemed more like hours, everyone in the TOC just stood or sat motionlessly and listened to the radio traffic. No one made any movement. Two ARVN soldiers in the TOC started crying. Finally, I got my emotions under control and, without realizing it at the time, took control of the ARVN/district TOC.

My interpreter, SFC Long, had heard the mortars landing near his home. He quickly dressed, left his family, and joined me in doing his job. What loyalty! Through him, I began giving assignments to each TOC member to gather certain types of information or sort out information we already had. We needed to determine the size of the NVA units at different locations and put together our assumptions of their primary objectives. Once everyone had a task to perform, the TOC began to function again. Capt. Nguyen looked at me, smiled, stood up, and resumed functioning as the operations officer. SFC Long and I left the TOC. I did not want them to see how much I was beginning to shake.

Where is Lt. Col. Thanh? He, more so than me, should be leading the defense of Mo Duc. I thought of going to his quarters myself but then remembered the stern warning I had received upon my arrival in June. No one was to approach the district chief's quarters unless specifically invited. Even after three months, I had never been invited. I thought better of the idea and decided to pass.

Staff Sgt. Jackson and Sandy, our second interpreter, returned to the team house. Jackson reported that many of the perimeter guards were preparing their breakfast over small campfires and were not too diligent regarding their perimeter duties.

It was time for me to prepare a hasty and limited situational report for the province advisor team. Province responded that they were receiving reports of NVA units and attacks in other districts, especially in Duc Pho, the adjoining district south of Mo Duc.

Mortar fire had decreased somewhat but never ceased. The Viet Cong were usually conservative with their ammunition expenditures. The mortars had been impacting for about an hour. Those mortars were not from the Viet Cong—another indication that we were being attacked by the NVA.

During recent morning briefings, Capt. Nguyen had routinely stated that approximately 105 territorial soldiers remained overnight within the district compound. This figure did not include three Americans and four Vietnamese considered as advisory team members. These units were three PF platoons and the sub-sector command structure. In addition, some civilian office workers (male and female) usually remained overnight, but not always. Six to eight National Police enroute somewhere north of Mo Duc had entered the district headquarters the previous evening. They requested and were granted permission to stay overnight and planned to depart in the morning.

0600 HOURS

After updating my higher headquarters on our situation via secure radio, I returned to the TOC where Capt. Nguyen and I quickly concluded, from the reports of those units attacked during the last hour or so, that all mortar barrages thus far had been followed up with a ground attack. Of course, I had to again acknowledge that his reports of NVA soldiers in western Mo Duc over the past several weeks had been accurate. Perhaps the district headquarters should expect a ground attack as well. We sure hoped not.

My team believed we could defend successfully because prudent preparations had been made by previous American advisor teams and local Vietnamese commanders over the years. Only the western perimeter seemed vulnerable as the refugee camp had been allowed to encroach toward our perimeter during the past two years. Also, a permanent schoolhouse was erected too close to the perimeter. At the time of its construction, it was on the edge of the hamlet. Now it seemed to be part of the refugee camp. The good news was that the Mo Duc district headquarters had never been attacked other than receiving harassing mortar fire from time to time.

Even so, we were genuinely concerned about the closeness of our western perimeter to the refugee camp and the schoolhouse. Too many of our important facilities were within a few yards of the western berm and perimeter wires. I suggested that Capt. Nguyen consider splitting his TOC with equal capabilities into two locations. The base of the tower seemed to be the safest place for another TOC. Nguyen seemed to agree but did nothing to indicate he would implement my suggestion.

Suddenly, the northwest perimeter erupted with outgoing small arms and machine gun fire. As I raced to the source of the firing, a hailstorm of incoming bullets began flying overhead and around me. I had never before been exposed to such a barrage of rifle fire. It was truly frightening!

I arrived at the northwest perimeter just as my team arrived. Fortified behind our small berm, we observed approximately 50 to 70 well-dressed uniformed soldiers half running and half sloshing through the rice paddies, firing at the perimeter as they approached. These were not poorly dressed Viet Cong; they were trained NVA soldiers. The water levels in the rice paddies were twice their normal levels and created a serious obstacle for these soldiers. My team and the PF platoon directed our firepower toward the advancing soldiers. Within 10 minutes, this small attacking force was repelled, with many of them killed and wounded.

This small attacking force wore mixed uniforms of all green, all black, and black and tan apparel. The water levels in the rice paddies slowed their advance and made them easy targets. Their attack seemed less than enthusiastic, somewhat half-hearted. The attackers did not act as if they were committed to their effort and never got closer than about 25 yards to our perimeter. This quick attack was more like a "turkey shoot" for us. All of us on the perimeter were amazed and confused by what had just taken place. The fact that the NVA soldiers were actually attacking the Mo Duc compound had a sobering effect on all the ARVN soldiers. Or, should I say, it was more of a wake-up call.

My team realized the PF/ARVN soldiers within our compound had expended almost all their ammunition on hand during that short firefight. Most of these relatively inexperienced ARVN soldiers were not aware of where additional ammunition was stored. These soldiers were also in various stages of dress, most scantily clad, since they had been waiting to go to the well for their routine morning bath. Others had been preparing breakfast over small campfires. In short, these men were not prepared for a determined ground attack from a well-trained enemy force.

I instructed Staff Sgt. Jackson and my interpreters to lead soldiers to the ammunition storage locations and distribute most of the ammo to the perimeter in case of another attack. They were also directed to encourage the ARVN to get into uniform and be prepared.

Back in the TOC, I saw that the district chief had finally arrived. I briefed him about all I had witnessed and the actions I had taken, but he seemed indifferent to my briefing. I was not sure how to react to his indifference, but honestly, I had not been impressed by his character or leadership since I arrived in Mo Duc anyway. Perhaps he thought I had overstepped my authority. Maybe so, but where was he when decisions needed to be made? It might be best that I stayed out of the TOC for a while… and out of sight, too.

Lt. Col. Nguyen Van Thanh, the ARVN district chief, and Major Bill Collier are pictured here at Team 17 Province Headquarters in Quang Ngai City during the July 4th celebrations for the Americans. July 4, 1972. Photo provided by Col. Bill Collier.

0700 HOURS

The RF 183 company on the Nui Khoang tactical OP reported that they were being overrun. After that radio transmission, no further radio communication was possible. Almost all of the friendly force personnel were killed and some captured, according to reports from the refugee camp.

Harassing mortar fire and sniper fire directed on or near our compound/district headquarters was intermittent at that point.

0800 HOURS

A large NVA force was observed moving into the heavy tree line 100 meters south of district headquarters. Later an NVA prisoner of war report implied that this battalion belonged to the 52nd NVA Regiment of the 2nd NVA Division.

Intelligence reports later revealed that the NVA battalion was several hours late moving into position. They were supposed to have been the primary attacking force from the south in the earlier ground attack. This was another fortunate occurrence—or blessing, as I considered it to be. The small attacking force from the northwest was designated as a diversionary force designed to split our meager response. Had this NVA battalion arrived on time and attacked at 0600 hours, the outcome of the battle for Mo Duc might have been quite different. We were not prepared to fight a large force at 0600 hours. In all likelihood, the district headquarters compound would have been completely overrun.

0900 HOURS

The TOC continued receiving a high volume of radio reports from various military locations. The district hamlet of Dong Cat, the nearby hamlets of Thiet Troung, Quang Hien, Nui Khoang, and the refugee center directly west of the district headquarters were now occupied by NVA combat units. The PF platoons fought courageously but were simply overwhelmed by the strength of the enemy forces.

The district headquarters was completely surrounded, with the enemy no further away than 100 meters and 20 meters at the closest point. I saw fear in the eyes of many of our soldiers, especially those on the perimeter. They were nearly petrified by the sightings of so many NVA soldiers.

And they were not the only ones scared. My team, including me, had a heavy feeling of helplessness at that time. Undesirable weather was also against us. The typhoon weather was preventing us from obtaining any outside support or assistance whatsoever.

I climbed to the third level of the concrete tower built by the French. This tower allowed unobstructed 360-degree observation for at least five miles. I could see the South China Sea five miles to the east from the tower. From the observation tower location, looking westward, I saw more NVA soldiers than I ever wanted to see, many of them in the refugee camp and at the schoolhouse. This viewing simply served to verify reports that we were completely surrounded. It became obvious that the district headquarters compound was the primary target of the 52nd NVA Regiment. Allegedly, over 1,000 troops were committed to overrun the district headquarters at this time. Another 1,000-plus troops were close by and throughout many of the villages and hamlets of Mo Duc district. I asked Capt. Nguyen how many soldiers we had inside our compound. He said, "About 120 counting your team." I realized quite clearly that this was *not* going to be a fair fight.

Everyone in the district compound was on full alert now. An understanding of the gravity of our situation was clear and apparent. We were painfully aware that, in all likelihood, we would not be able to successfully defend against another attack by this large, well-trained, and determined NVA force. We did not have a sufficient number of soldiers compared to those opposing us, our supply of ammunition was limited, we had no external fire support available, and I feared that the NVA level of training was probably superior to that of our Vietnamese soldiers. It was simply overwhelming (and terrifying) to even consider the odds we faced. The battle line was set. The radio reports from several units indicated that the NVA was not interested in taking many prisoners.

1000–1200 HOURS

The advisor team spent most of the morning dodging intermittent sniper and machine gun fire while on the perimeter, encouraging the ARVN soldiers and PF platoon soldiers to be vigilant for possible ground attacks. I walked the perimeter numerous times during the morning. It was nerve-wracking to know you were going to be attacked, yet not know precisely when, from which direction, how many enemy soldiers would be participating, their variety of weapons, and their specific objectives in our compound.

Several limited ground assaults were attempted by the NVA against our west, northwest, and southern perimeters during the morning but were easily repelled. When their probing attacks occurred, several members of my team or I immediately responded and returned small arms fire. We also made almost immediate personnel adjustments to strengthen that location, and the NVA quickly ceased their probing attack in response. I did not realize what they were doing at the time, but looking back, I believe they were probably probing to test our defenses, watching how we responded, and noting our resolve to fight.

Quang Ngai province had been a Viet Minh communist stronghold against the French during the late 1940s and 1950s. Mo Duc is the ancestral home of the then-North Vietnamese Premier Pham Van Dong. Many believed that the people of Mo Duc and Quang Ngai would rise up against the South Vietnam government when given the chance. If this were to happen, now would be the time.

We knew that the typhoon had eliminated the possibility of tactical air support and naval gunfire. But we were in dire need of some external fire support. I requested availability of any ARVN artillery from surrounding districts through my radio communications and asked Capt. Nguyen to do the same through his channels. By this time, it was a well-known fact that Mo Duc was under attack district-wide. I did not know how much effort my higher headquarters had exerted to get me some external support, or even if any external support had been identified.

Sometimes, the lack of knowing even one way or another is depressing.

Suddenly, I noticed someone was calling me on the radio. His call sign had the word "angel" in it. That is all I can remember now. When he keyed his mic, I could hear the distinct sounds of a Huey. He had a flight of two aircraft and was enroute to retrieve my advisory team. That was wonderful news. I did not know helicopters were in the area! I believed he was from the Da Nang area. So, my higher headquarters *was* trying to get me some help. That was encouraging but, in truth, was to no avail at that time. I thanked him for his mission to take us out of Mo Duc and told him I was not going to leave, even if I could.

After explaining our situation and telling him it would be suicide for them to land at Mo Duc, he ignored me and said, "Don't worry, sir, we will get you out of there." I replied that my helipad was located outside of the compound and would accommodate only one Huey at a time. Furthermore, I replied—and I still remember my exact words to this day—"If you land on my helipad, I will not leave the compound and get on your chopper. If you land, you will be shot up and not be able to lift off."

Again, he seemed to ignore me, telling me not to worry. He would get us.

Now the weather was still light rain with low clouds. I was searching the northern skies for him. I even had a red flare to pop when he got near, preparing to tell him to immediately abort the mission. *Do not land.*

Then I saw them.

There they were, flying low at about 1,000 feet. Mortars started landing about that time. The chopper pilot called again. This time, he said, "I see what you mean. We will not land. Sorry, we cannot get you any longer. Good luck, sir." And the two Hueys turned east and flew out over the South China Sea, then turning north to head back from wherever they had come. I was thankful they did not try to land. At the same time, it was gratifying to know that those Americans were willing to risk their lives to save Staff Sgt. Jackson and me.

The team's primary radios were located in the team house radio room. The roof was made of simple orange clay tiles, as they were on all Vietnamese/French structures. At some point in the morning, a mortar round came through the radio room roof and destroyed the team's primary communication radios. We only had a few backup radios in the team house. From that time on, I carried a PRC-25 radio on my back.

I moved most of my undamaged equipment to the base of the tower, which provided my team with a safer environment from which to operate. I returned to the TOC with my two interpreters and looked for the district chief. I was told he had left the TOC hours ago and that he had not issued any orders or changed any instructions. I guessed that was good, but unusual for a commander, I thought.

I told Capt. Nguyen we would help him move some of his TOC to the base of the tower. He seemed slow to respond until we started actually picking up his radios and other equipment. Then he agreed, and we soon had two functional TOCs. A few hours after relocating the TOC, an NVA mortar round partially destroyed the original TOC. The district was back to one fully functional TOC again, but it was now located in the base of the tower.

With the strong likelihood that we would eventually be overrun, it became imperative that all U.S. encryption codebooks be destroyed by burning them. The province advisor team was notified of my decision to burn these books and all pertinent team files in our team office when I could safely do so. They did not object to this decision, and I used a cut-off 55-gallon drum to burn all the paper files in the advisor filing cabinets.

Sniper fire was becoming more effective, and the ARVN casualties were increasing. The dispensary had only a few basic medical supplies, and there was no trained Vietnamese medic available to care for the wounded. My team medic, Bassinett, was still in Quang Ngai City. For numerous ARVN causalities, their medical care was basic without any physician or medic to administer pain relief medicines to relieve their agony. I encouraged Capt. Nguyen to insist that all wounded still able to fire a weapon remain at their post in their perimeter positions.

Many did.

NOON–1500 HOURS

During infrequent lulls in small arms and sniper fire, I began burning seven years of sensitive and classified Vietnamese operational and advisory reports detailing all aspects of American support in the district of Mo Duc. These reports in the team filing cabinets included the names of village and hamlet chiefs and many others who cooperated with the Americans. If these files had fallen into NVA possession, numerous South Vietnamese officials would have surely been assassinated. Unfortunately, I burned these files in the open near the flagpole, and it became a popular target for the machine gunner in Dong Cat. This burning effort was time-consuming, and amid numerous interruptions, was successfully completed by nightfall.

Sammy, one of my bodyguards, finally located the machine gunner's firing position. He seemed to be semi-exposed yet also with some cover. To engage this gunner, Sammy had to position himself behind a very low berm on the east-side perimeter while being pretty much exposed. When the machine gunner opened fire, Sammy seemed to take delight in returning fire. Usually, the machine gunner would remain silent for a while.

While burning the paper files, I noticed approximately eight soldiers in a small group not too far from the flagpole and the main gate. Capt. Nguyen arrived about this time, pointed to the group, and said they were the National Police soldiers who had stopped by the previous day for an overnight visit. They had just told him they were leaving and going out the main gate. They were terrified by the sight of the massing NVA and spoke of desertion and surrender. Other ARVN soldiers were gathering to see if the National Police were allowed to leave. I had no intention of allowing anyone to depart the compound or surrender.

SFC Long, my interpreter, was nearby, as he always was. We walked over to talk with the National Police. I explained in no uncertain terms that anyone who left the compound had valuable information about our strength and casualties. Everyone in the compound was needed at that moment to help with our defense. I stressed that no one would leave the compound alive by firing numerous rounds from my M16 rifle near but to the side of them. They understood my message and returned to their perimeter positions.

I continued burning files. Suddenly, the machine gunner decided that I was his next target. He was becoming an irritation. Sammy came running to engage this gunner. Since I was his target, I decided that it should be my turn to attempt to neutralize this NVA gunner. After emptying a magazine into his location and no longer receiving a response, I returned to burning files.

A short time later, Capt. Nguyen sought me out on the perimeter. He had a big smile on his face. He could hardly wait to tell me some good news. Two 105-mm howitzers of ARVN artillery from Tu Nghia, the district directly north of Mo Duc, had been positioned either on their southern border or just inside the Mo Duc district. I was overjoyed. The Province Advisor headquarters provided this same information a few minutes after Nguyen's notification. Mo Duc district headquarters would be near the howitzers' maximum firing range; therefore, some erratic rounds could be expected. These howitzers were our sole source of external fire support at this time. We were relieved to have some external fire support, even if it was of limited value due to its maximum range.

Mortar and rocket positions were located to the west and south of district headquarters. Enemy forces had dug in static defensive positions with overhead cover in Dong Cat. The strongest probing assaults were launched from the southwest and west of district headquarters. Each probing assault resulted in a reduction of our small arms ammunition and often several more ARVN casualties. I wondered if the NVA realized they were seriously reducing our ammunition and personnel resources.

We were becoming accustomed to intermittent small arms fire, automatic weapons fire, indirect and direct fire, which included 82mm mortar, 120mm mortar, and 122mm rockets. Every so often, a much larger caliber weapon impacted near our compound in the rice paddies or near the Dong Cat hamlet. The rounds were erratic. I thought they were 105mm howitzer rounds being fired from LZ Dragon by NVA soldiers who were not trained cannoneers as most of the rounds went astray. The district compound had one 81mm mortar in a protected mortar pit but with limited overhead protection. I provided coordinates of the suspected howitzer location to Nguyen and directed him to have the mortar crew fire on LZ Dragon, with the hopes of damaging whatever was firing at our compound. The firing stopped for a short period of time. Later I learned that some of my ARVN soldiers believed it was a 106mm recoilless rifle.

Nowhere seemed safe. Whether out in the open burning files, on one of the perimeters, in the tower base TOC, or on the third level of the tower, some type of enemy firepower was entering the district compound. There was no doubt that the NVA was keeping a close watch on our movements in the compound. Eventually, they figured out that I was a key person based on how active I was. They knew when I was in the upper tower and began shooting at me, with some rounds entering through the gun ports and ricocheting around. I asked Capt. Nguyen to send me a good marksman to return fire from the tower with me. The marksman stayed with me wherever I went during the remainder of the battle.

When the large caliber weapon began firing again, I asked Capt. Nguyen to provide the grid coordinates of LZ Dragon and the Nui Khoang plateau in a request for an artillery shower for the NVA soldiers at those locations. In retrospect, this artillery shower may have been the reason the 105mm captured by the NVA stopped firing for a period of time. I am not sure the artillery reached the actual coordinates given. I am sure they got the message, however. This reasoning was nothing more than pure conjecture by me.

From the observation tower, I was able to see a few potential targets to the north. To the west was the crowded refugee camp and hamlet all the way to LZ Dragon. No targets were visible there other than one and probably two NVA battalions intermingled with the refugees. Any targets south of my position were out of the range of the Tu Nghia artillery. I adjusted the artillery on several suspected enemy locations north of my location with some limited success. My PRC-25 radio transmission range was limited and insufficient to communicate with the ARVN artillery location. To accomplish this mission, I passed my subsequent artillery corrections to SFC Long, who hollered them down to the TOC in the tower base. We got the job done this way. As expected, range and deflection dispersion were significant.

Upon realizing that we now had artillery support, the ARVN and PF soldiers demanded that we fire into the refugee camp to neutralize the battalion NVA threat there. From the moment I heard their demand, I knew this was something I did not want to do. Why? No one actually knew the number of people in the refugee camp. But it had an exceptionally large population, with approximately 15,000 to 20,000 or more people. And the shacks they called home were next to each other with minimal separation between them. That camp was extremely crowded and it had to be uncomfortable for everyone living there. Only one road existed wide enough for a two-and-a-half-ton truck to travel through the camp from MSR 1 to LZ Dragon. A shallow stream ran alongside the road. Women washed clothes in that stream, kids played in and around it, and yes, I observed people urinating in it from time to time.

I would travel on that road two or three times each week to visit the units on the Nui Khoang plateau. Often, we (my interpreter and I) would speak with the children using my elementary Vietnamese. The children loved to hear me speak their language and laughed, pointing at me and jumping around, making sounds. I should have been offended. However, SFC Long said that their interaction with me was positive and that they actually understood most of what I said. When you mess up a tone in the Vietnamese language, it sometimes changes the entire meaning of the sentence, which can be humorous. The women were reluctant to talk with me at first. Soon, several did. It was rare to see a teenage or middle-aged male in the camp during the day. We had to assume they were working in the rice paddies.

A box of C-rations was usual cargo in our jeep when we traveled in the district. At first, I gave the children some C-ration goodies, mostly meals I did not like but they did. On one particular trip to Nui Khoang, I was eating a C-ration while we drove through the refugee camp. Some of the children wanted to talk and eventually wanted a C-ration. I showed them how to use the P-38 (a can opener for C-rations). Much to my surprise, several of them already knew. Apparently, I was not the first American to share C-rations with them. Four of us had lunch together that day. Eating with them became a weekly event by August 1972. Several women took C-rations too but would not eat with me. Furthermore, many of my Vietnamese soldiers had families in the hamlets, which now were entangled with the refugee camp. I was told that they saw the need to get the NVA out of those locations and reluctantly agreed to shooting the artillery as a solution. I did not think they had thought this action through as much as they should have.

Firing at targets in the refugee camp that were difficult to see may have reduced the threat to us inside the district compound. By doing so, though, we most likely would have killed and wounded hundreds of innocent civilian children and adults. Doing this had no military or moral value whatsoever, in my opinion. After a short period of reflecting on their demand and my experiences with some of the camp inhabitants, I knew I could not give the order or even allow someone else to give the order to fire into the refugee camp. This was an extremely intense decision for me, especially considering the pressures from all sides and the potential disastrous human impact. I told Nguyen we were not to fire into the refugee camp under any circumstances. We had to determine another way to deal with our critical situation.

Many of the ARVN soldiers were upset with me, and they let me know how they felt. At that point, I faced the enemy from outside the compound and from inside the compound as well. Several told me that I had sealed their fate, that my decision would cause all of us inside the compound to die. Many were also worried about what would happen to their families if we were overrun. I asked them what would happen to their families if we fired artillery into and throughout the hamlet and refugee camp. It was a no-win situation for them *and* for me.

Now I had to watch my back inside the compound. Morally, I was willing to accept my fate based on my decision.

1500–1800 HOURS

At 1540, a crowning blow to my day occurred. I could not find Staff Sgt. Jackson or Sandy anywhere on the perimeter. *Perhaps they were in the team bunker,* I thought. As I was approaching the team bunker, approximately four to six feet from the bunker entrance door, a 122mm rocket on fuze delay penetrated the bunker and exploded several feet below the ceiling. The force of the explosion knocked me into the team house wall. I had never been that close to an exploding artillery shell. The expanding air created by the explosion was amazing. I think I may have lost consciousness for a brief period. I remember lying next to the wall, picking up my helmet, and noticing several areas of blood from minor injuries to my body, apparently caused by the explosion. Smoke billowed out of the bunker. Seeing the smoke, I quickly regained my sense of where I was.

If this had happened to me outside the bunker, what had happened inside the bunker?

My two bodyguards and I entered the bunker and found Jackson dead. Also killed were my other interpreter, Sandy, and his dog. Small fires were burning inside the bunker, and almost everything was destroyed. The antenna of my PRC-25 radio was broken when the explosion knocked me to the wall and the ground, and my right ear was bleeding from the inside, probably caused by a concussion. I replaced the broken antenna with a makeshift antenna using a coat hanger, which worked sufficiently but with reduced range. I radioed province headquarters and informed them of what had happened. I reiterated our need for external fire support.

Things were going from bad to worse. I was the only American alive in the district headquarters, and I seemed to be the one in control of everything. The loss of Jackson and Sandy, increasing casualties, and the realization that a larger enemy assault force loomed, along with a rapidly diminishing supply of small arms ammunition and no help from sources outside our compound. We were limited to two tubes of ARVN artillery whose rounds could barely reach us and could not reach the west beyond the refugee camp or south of the compound. Many of my ARVN soldiers were also clearly unhappy with me. All these factors combined painted a less than rosy picture. To be truthful, a feeling of hopelessness was quickly clouding my mind.

I could not have felt any more helpless than I did at that moment. What does one do when one sees no hope whatsoever?

They pray. And pray I did.

I turned the battle over to God, praying for the safety and wellbeing of my wife and children in the United States, praying not to become a prisoner of war, acknowledging that I could die here, and praying to die honorably. I left everything up to Him and asked that His Will be done.

Surely, there had to be a solution or sufficient help necessary to survive this situation. Then I became the target of psychological warfare. In near perfect English, a voice came over my radio, speaking my name very clearly and informing me I had no chance of withstanding their assaults and should surrender immediately. Otherwise, I was going to die. Upon hearing my name spoken by someone who had an accent similar to my interpreters, I was elated, expecting to hear some good news that help was on the way. My elation quickly turned to depression as he spoke.

He went on to say that I would never see my wife Patricia (he called her by her name) and children again. He said another man would raise and discipline my children, and that man would occupy my wife's bed. He reiterated these statements and more several times. All I had to do was surrender. That voice threatened me with the presence of thousands of well-trained and prepared soldiers surrounding me, eager to rid South Vietnam of a corrupt government. He continued by saying that I must realize by now that the Peoples' Army troops had control of the entire district of Mo Duc. If I were to surrender the headquarters now, I could go free and return home to my family. I believe his intention was to lessen my morale. And it worked… but only for a few minutes.

Why was he asking me to surrender the headquarters instead of asking the district chief?

This may have been a defining moment for me. Little did the voice over the radio realize that the result of his banter was to incense me to the point that I was determined to survive no matter what. At the worst, they may have killed me eventually, but I intended to take as many of them with me as I could. I did not respond to his radio message, hoping he would think I had not heard him.

During previous years, the Civil Operations and Revolutionary Development Support (CORDS) Program, a pacification effort by the U.S. government, had provided local Vietnamese governments with Motorola radios that, in the 1960s, cost $25 apiece. Many had been issued to districts, villages, and some hamlet chiefs in Mo Duc to aid in their village security and administration projects. Unbeknownst to me, Capt. Nguyen also had several of these radios and had been receiving activity/intelligence reports from numerous villages and hamlets throughout the day. He had great communication with civilian authorities via Motorola radios and military units via tactical radios. However, at that time, and in several instances due to the combat situation, they were co-located.

My refusal to shoot artillery at the NVA battalion or battalions intermingled with the people in the refugee camp was quickly transmitted via the civilian Motorola radios.

Once my decision found its way to the refugee camp and the adjoining village and hamlets, a miracle happened. These people knew exactly where the various units of the 52nd NVA regiment were located outside their civilian populations. Suddenly, our TOC was being provided the locations of NVA mortar positions, artillery and rocket positions, field aid stations, troop concentrations, and even the location of the regimental commander's field headquarters.

One target's location was a nice house by local standards, where an NVA battalion commander had established his headquarters. One of the ARVN soldiers in the TOC exclaimed that the house was inhabited by a relative of North Vietnamese Prime Minister Pham Van Dong. Most of the locations were west and south of our district headquarters. I plotted many of the locations on my map and then went up the tower to visually try to spot them. Of course, most of the targets were beyond the range of the Tu Nghia artillery. There were many targets with no means to neutralize them.

All was quiet for an hour or so, and I wondered what they were planning next. The absence of mortars and small arms and crew-served weapons firing was eerie. *Maybe they no longer thought that taking the district compound was worth it.* We had already inflicted heavy personnel casualties on them, and they had control of most of the district's land.

1800-2200 HOURS

They were planning something. We soon found out when they attacked the western perimeter that this was *not* a probing assault. The western open area was full of NVA soldiers—hundreds of them. They were shouting and making a lot of noise. There was precious little time to respond, much less reallocate people and ammo. The PF platoon and National Police Field Force platoon defending the district jail and west perimeter were partially overrun. NVA forces penetrated the perimeter and occupied the military dispensary, jail, and school in the northwest corner. I ordered most of those hanging around the tower TOC to follow me to the western wall to help repel them. Hand-to-hand fighting was already occurring.

As I rounded one of the building corners, an NVA soldier was approaching from the opposite direction. We both fired our pistols at the other, and I turned and ran back around the corner. As he did not seem to chase me, he was probably waiting for me to poke my head back around the corner. I wanted to go back around the corner, as it was the shortest distance to where I believed the penetration had occurred. For whatever reason, I decided to take a different route to the perimeter, choosing to go by our mortar pit instead. This route actually provided me with a better view of the penetration. It became obvious that we were outnumbered. We were losing the fight and would soon be completely overrun. I felt that my only recourse was to call for artillery on our western perimeter.

I ran back to the TOC and told Capt. Nguyen to have the Tu Nghia artillery fire low air bursts on our position. Then we told our guys to take cover. The fighting continued until two air bursts occurred. More of the NVA were injured than my ARVN soldiers were, and thankfully, the NVA retreated. Those low air bursts and the concussion from the 122mm rocket explosion inside the team bunker are the primary reasons I wear hearing aids today.

Later that evening, my ARVN soldiers presented me with a 9mm Chinese communist pistol with a star symbol on both sides of the handgrip and a holster with a cleaning rod that belonged to an NVA officer. I now knew why that NVA soldier did not chase me. He was a 1st lieutenant.

Tokarev pistol, Type 54. Developed in the 1930s by Soviet weapons designer Fedor Tokarev and designated Type 51, adopted by the Chinese in 1951, and used both Soviet and Chinese parts. When China began manufacturing the weapon without Soviet parts in 1954, the designation was changed to Type 54. The star in the handgrips represents the Communist Party star. It is available in both 7.62x25mm and 9x19mm.

An abundance of 9mm ammunition was captured by my ARVN troops during the battle. During the next two months, I carried this Tokarev Type 54 pistol as my personal sidearm and willingly returned their 9mm ammunition one round at a time to the extent of available NVA and Viet Cong targets. "Fair is fair," as the saying goes.

Lt. Col. Thanh, the district chief, was now well situated in the rear of the TOC located in the tower base. He had at least three ARVN soldiers watching him constantly and catering to his every need. He would not participate in any battle-related discussions. His demeanor was quiet, which was different from his normal behavior. Like a blinding glimpse of the obvious, I suddenly realized that Capt. Nguyen and others in the TOC were seeking and taking orders from me rather than the district chief. This is *not* the way the TOC should operate. I remember thinking that this would become an issue when and if we survived the battle. But at that moment in time, survival was the all-important issue. I had been taught that "when in charge, be in charge." From that point forward, I functioned as the only commander in the compound, whether the district chief was present or not.

I was handed a bowl of warm rice. After three months of eating with the Vietnamese, I usually enjoyed eating rice. I just could not eat much at that time. Looking back, I cannot remember eating or drinking much until September 18.

Via civilian Motorola radio, we learned that there were some survivors from the LZ Dragon attack (which had taken place at 0500) who wanted to enter our compound but did not want to get shot by us while doing so. The sun was setting as my guys provided covering fire while the survivors ran across the 30 or 40 yards of open area to our main gate. I watched two surviving artillerymen, three survivors from the RF 183 CO, and two survivors from the 1/30 RF CO group safely and joyfully enter our compound. These brave men had fought their way through enemy lines while employing escape and evasion measures to arrive at the district headquarters compound. What a feat they had performed. I wondered if they realized how hopeless our situation was. They had gone from the frying pan into the fire.

The tempo of mortar rounds, small arms, and crew-served weapons fire increased. It was not all directed at our compound. Mortars were landing at various locations one or two miles from us, sometimes closer. Capt. Nguyen said he thought soldiers of the various RF companies and PF platoons were still trying to fight. This could have been the case. *It was going to be a long night.*

Two large caliber rounds were fired toward us. Could they be coming from the 105mm howitzer? We countered by firing a single mortar onto LZ Dragon.

At dusk each evening, it was our policy to turn on the perimeter lights. Sammy, one of the bodyguards who also performed most of the minor maintenance for the team, usually did this and felt that he should turn on the lights that evening as well. Within minutes of the lights coming on, NVA sharpshooters in Dong Cat shot out the lightbulbs on that side of the perimeter. Sammy had a supply of lightbulbs. Retrieving the bulbs along with a ladder, Sammy began climbing up the ladder and replacing the bulbs. While replacing the bulbs, he was wounded in both legs. SFC Long and I found Sammy in a building closer to the compound center, which was being used as a dispensary/morgue. Sammy greeted us with his usual broad smile when he saw us and then, almost crying, apologized for getting shot and being unable to replace the perimeter lights. After all we had been through during this day and then seeing Sammy's reaction, I knew I was surrounded by some incredible human beings.

2200–2400 HOURS

The tempo of mortar rounds, small arms, and crew-served weapons fire did not seem to decrease much as I recall now, although it all was not directed at the district compound. Over my radio, a voice called out, "Mike 36." That was my call sign. The voice then identified himself as "Covey 100." That was Capt. Joseph A. Personett, USAF. With him was "Covey 111," Capt. Richard L. Poling, also USAF.

What was covey? After a brief explanation, I learned these guys were two USAF forward aircraft controllers (FACs) flying in an OV-10 Bronco aircraft. The cloudy weather conditions, if nothing else, would probably preclude good and accurate target location. The weather had improved some during the evening. After briefing them on my situation, Capt. Personett said they would help as best they could, and, of course, I readily accepted their help.

In 2014, I was made aware of an article entitled "Point of the Spear" written in 2003 by Capt. Joseph A. Personett and published in the Covey FAC Association publication in 2003. This lengthy article describes much of his and Covey 111's (Capt. Poling) involvement in the Battle for Mo Duc. Following is a portion of that article:

> *I had been on quick launch alert that night with the 20th TASS at Da Nang. I was quietly playing liar's dice in the smoke TASS Hole Bar while sipping my Ginger Ale. I was expecting to go to bed soon, just as soon as I had taken everyone's money. Just one more round should have done it. I was winning for a change, largely due to the fact that I was still sober, while everyone else had been consuming large numbers of Heinekens all night long. None other than the squadron intelligence officer prematurely destroyed the consummation of my perfect plan to liberate my fellow FACs of all their money. He came storming into the TASS Hole out of breath with his fat fingers clutching a FRAG order for a Troops in Contact (TIC) engagement somewhere down south of Quang Ngai. I thought he was kidding since nothing had been fragged down south for the 20th TASS in months. There was a nasty typhoon lingering off the coast and most of the aircraft in I and II Corps had been evacuated to Thailand.*
>
> *He huffed and puffed while explaining that I had to get going now due to the dire straits of the ARVN outfit that was reporting they were about to be overrun. I finally sensed that he really was serious about this and could possibly be telling the truth.*
>
> *I stated to him that two FACs were required for a night mission and that I was the only one left on duty. That was when Rich stepped up and said he would go with me in my back seat, even though he had already*

flown earlier that day and was not on duty. Rich had not been drinking Ginger Ale that night and I already had most of his money anyway.

At the formal intelligence briefing I was shocked to find out that the 105 fire support base really was in the process of being overrun. The weather at Mo Duc was really 'delta sierra' with high winds, low visibility due to torrential rains, and low ceilings right down to hilltop levels. We would probably not be able to see our targets unless we were below the cloud bases of 1500 to 2500 feet. We also found out that most if not all of the close air support was moved out of Vietnam to Ubon, Thailand, to wait out the typhoon. What I did not know and forgot to ask, was the fact that all the rescue helicopters had moved to Thailand as well. We did not know that there were not Jolly Green Rescue helicopters in I or II Corps. We were told we would probably be on our own if and when we got to Mo Duc. What we carried to the fight was what we would probably be able to use there. Under the Rules of Engagement, since a TIC had already been declared., I could use my guns, however I thought strafing at night was risky business at best because doing it meant you had a pretty good chance of flying into the ground while you were lining up to shoot. The Willie Pete's we normally carried were useless for close in work with TIC's except to mark the targets for the fighters. Fighters would probably not be available tonight due to the weather. No fast movers wanted to work below anything lower than a 10,000 ft ceiling.

I decided to download the Willie Pete's on the alert bird and reload flechettes into the LAU pods. Four pods filled with twenty-eight 2.75 flechettes rockets should stop what we thought was a limited Viet Cong attacking on the fire support base. This was my thinking by the end of the intelligence briefing.

South of Quang Ngai we started picking up the FM radio conversations of the grunts. There were at least two American Special Forces with the ARVN unit at Mo Duc. They were there to train and advise them as well as act as communications officers in time of need. It was a time of need, and they were communicating with the world. It seems that all hell was breaking out around Mo Duc. The firebase had been overrun. It was not a company of VC but a battalion of NVA regulars. Highway One was blocked by NVA forces both north and south of Mo Duc, so that ARVN ground reinforcements could not get through to help the Mo Duc defenders. The weather was bad with low ceilings, but not as bad as the briefing indicated. We were over the overcast and could see the glow of the Mo Duc firefight down below us. There were lots of house fires both in the town and the refugee camp. Suddenly a line of fire streaked out below us lighting up the night. It was a 105 firing at the compound. We had to do something now to stop the ensuing carnage. Do we take a chance and go down below the overcast and maybe hit high terrain or stay up above and wait for the weather to break? Another round went off.

Then I heard something that made my decision easy. It was not what the SF grunt said, but how he said it and the tone in his voice. He knew he was going to die if the guns were not immediately silenced, and he let us know it by the resolve in his voice. It was almost as if he was saying goodbye to us. As if he was saying, 'Thanks for trying to save us and we know you cannot do anything because of the weather.' That was all it took. Pray Rich, I am going in.

That large caliber weapon had just fired a few more rounds. Unfortunately, their accuracy was improving. I described the suspected location of the captured 105mm howitzer or 106mm recoilless rifle and asked the OV-10 pilots to silence the weapon. Almost immediately, Capt. Personett acknowledged the target location. I believe they had some help as it fired again. They spotted it firing and rolled in on that location. The large caliber weapon never fired at us again.

Thank you, United States Air Force.

But there is more to their story. These two FACs, with the help of two F-4s with Mark 82s out of Ubon, Thailand, diverted to them from up north just for this. "Troops in contact" (TIC) permanently silenced the 105mm howitzer. I was told they were Marine F-4s stationed in Thailand.

I began providing target coordinates from the list provided to me by the villagers earlier in the day. The FACs went straight to work on them. They visually saw mortars and artillery firing at my compound and other friendly units. In all cases, Captains Personett and Poling expertly, successfully, and courageously attacked these positions with the weapons on their OV-10. At some point, close air support jet aircraft arrived over Mo Duc, and the FACs would direct them to a target.

From my position, where I was able to maintain an overview of the battlefield, I adjusted ARVN artillery and assisted the FACs in adjusting airstrikes using additional target locations based on my observations or sometimes from receiving good intelligence from the village and hamlet elders. As an artillery second lieutenant, I had adequate experience as a forward observer at Fort Sill, OK, and later served as a 105mm howitzer battery commander for eight months supporting the First Cavalry Division in 1966-1967 in Vietnam. To a certain degree, I was in my comfort zone, so to speak.

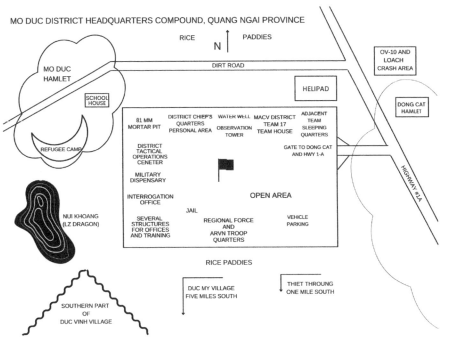

Hand-drawn depiction of structure relative locations inside the district headquarters compound and approximate locations of several key geographic areas important to the attack on the District Headquarters.

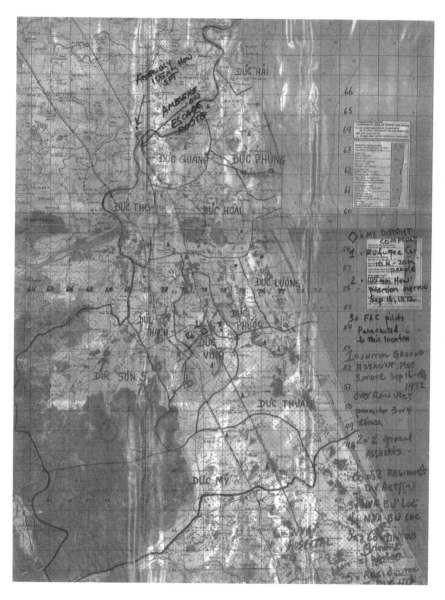

Maj. Bill Collier's Mo Duc battlefield map illustrating enemy locations around the tiny district compound, September 16-18, 1972. Map provided by Col. Bill Collier.

CHAPTER NINE
THE BATTLE FOR MO DUC,
SECOND DAY

17 SEPTEMBER 1972, SUNDAY
MIDNIGHT–0130 HOURS

There was plenty of work for the FACs, as this was a target-rich environment. I adjusted their target strikes based on my observations from my vantage point in the tower or from receiving good intelligence from the ARVN troops and the village elders over their cheap Motorola radios. The cloud cover was miraculously lifting, and the FACs were getting some improved visibility from limited explosions. Soon, the level of Northern Vietnamese Army (NVA) small arm and crew-served weapons activity decreased. We were in another lull except for incoming mortar rounds. No complaints, though. They were loud and scary, but not too accurate.

0130–0330 HOURS

A U.S. Navy destroyer, the USS Hanson (DD/DDR-832), contacted me and said it was ready to assist in any way it could. I thought I was hallucinating. I ran to the top of the tower, looked to the east, where the South China Sea was some four-plus miles away, and saw the faint silhouette of a beautiful destroyer sitting quietly offshore. I was born and raised in a Navy town and could usually immediately identify most Naval vessels. What a wonderful boost to my morale, and just when I needed it! I believe the destroyer's call sign was "Black Velvet." The USS Hanson later received the Meritorious Unit Commendation for providing Naval gunfire to allied forces in RVN. In the ship's award citation, it read, "The ship was cited for her accurate and timely gunfire causing significant damage to the enemy and is credited as a contributor with saving the district capital of Mo Duc from being overrun during the period of 16 and 17 September 1972."

In 2012, I searched the Internet for information about the USS Hanson. In the ship's "stories drop down," I found a great story by Dennis R. Wappes. Among his several stories was one relating to the Battle for Mo Duc.

Wappes wrote the following story:

My all-time most memorable moment of Vietnam was when I had just gone to bed and was awakened by the messenger telling me the captain wanted to see me on the bridge. I thought, 'What did I do now?' I raced to the bridge worried that I was in trouble. When I got there, the captain took me out on the starboard wing, put his arm around me like a father and said, 'Son, we have a problem.' He then explained to me that a message had been received about the Village of Mo Duc being under siege by enemy troops and that we had to get there with no time to spare to provide gunfire support. He told me that he had heard I was the finest helmsman aboard the ship and that he only trusts me to steer the ship through a minefield along coral reefs. He told me that if I went as much as ½ a degree off course, we would either hit a mine in one direction or the reef in the other. He did not order me to take the helm and told me that if I chose not to, a less time saving route would be planned and that I could go back to bed. He said, "The decision is up to you." I was moved by his approach and promptly took the helm. It was not until several years later that I learned of the lives that were saved by our timely arrival. That gave me a really good feeling deep down inside.

I believe the FACs adjusted naval gunfire for a relatively brief period. Then Covey 100 announced they were out of ordnance and low on fuel and were returning to Da Nang.

With the FACs gone, so would be the close air support. It did not take the NVA long to realize that the FACs and close air support were gone. NVA small arms and machine gun fire around our compound slowly increased, and it became more dangerous to observe from the berm or even the tower. I could not locate any targets within range for the ARVN artillery. Contact was re-established with the Navy, and I adjusted naval gunfire onto several targets. Observation was difficult that night. Adjusting naval or light artillery without good observation was difficult and could potentially do more harm than good. The last thing I wanted to do was injure friendly civilians with incorrect naval gunfire and potentially turn them against the ARVN. When the 2nd NVA Division entered Mo Duc, the civilian population did not rise up against the ARVN and South Vietnamese government as the communists had predicted.

I did not want to upset *that* apple cart.

In between naval gunfire missions, the silence was deafening. The waiting and wondering were playing on my nerves. I thought I would prefer they attack instead of this seemingly prolonged anticipation. Then I remembered the various target lists I had made earlier when the villagers were providing me with so much information. One of the targets had piqued my interest earlier, but the closer battle had my attention then. The villagers had provided the alleged location of the NVA division headquarters, several locations with NVA command and staff, small troop assembly areas, and their field dispensary or hospital. At this early hour of the morning, I had no way of knowing if these targets were still valid or if they had relocated. Chances were some had moved, and some had not.

As an experienced artilleryman and forward observer with hostile NVA soldiers surrounding me and a beautiful American naval destroyer sitting quietly offshore loaded with their big artillery projectiles, what was I to do other than continue to provide fire missions for the destroyer? It was my duty! These enemy locations were west and southwest of Mo Duc and LZ Dragon. Very few friendlies were in that area, and they had probably fled when the NVA arrived. The naval gunfire did a great job attacking these targets. Of course, I could not see their effects on the ground. I had to rely on field reports, mostly from civilians, relayed through several radios to surmise the effect on most targets. Using their responses, I would determine a correction and cross my fingers when the next round was fired. I had to be incredibly careful with my corrections, and it was a slower process than when adjusting light artillery. I was happy to hear their projectiles screaming above my location enroute to and impacting in the general area I had requested. Those projectiles passing overhead were like music to my ears. Days later, we learned that some large command and staff locations were hit. There is no doubt that Naval gunfire played a significant role in the survival of friendly forces during the Battle for Mo Duc.

Thank you, sailors of the USS Hanson.

Most of the enemy mortar positions were to the west and southwest and were infrequently active. The overall incoming fire seemed to have lessened but had not completely ceased. Maybe the NVA were running short on some of their ammo, or maybe they were just catching a few winks of sleep. I did not think any of us could have slept even if we had wanted to. And we were all exhausted. Any time you are being shot at or mortared or shelled, it is dangerous and worrisome. It is simply not the time to even try to take a nap. Instead, your mind is playing the "what if, when if, where if" game.

0330-0530 HOURS

Once again, it was mostly quiet. Suddenly, my radio came alive with the two FACs, Captains Personett and Poling. They were approaching Mo Duc in their refueled and rearmed OV-10 Bronco and wanted an update on the situation. Little did they realize how pleased I was with their return. They were my lifeline for survival. I was mentally jumping with joy. They could see areas and activities outside of my compound that I could not see, and they could bring tactical air support and resume naval gunfire to targets beyond my visual capability. They could also see inside the district compound and see activities occurring that I could not see or did not know were occurring. The FACs returned to the battle area over Mo Duc. When mortars fired, the FACs engaged their mortar positions. Slowly, the number of mortars firing in and around the district headquarters was being reduced.

Radio traffic had been minimal for quite a while. Just when I began to think the NVA had thought better of continuing the attack on the Mo Duc headquarters, radio traffic started to significantly increase. Incoming reports indicated troop movements taking place throughout the villages/hamlets and refugee camp. Were they preparing to depart under the cover of darkness? Capt. Nguyen could not get a confirmation or an indication of what was actually occurring, particularly throughout the areas west of our location. Covey was still above us and working, although they seemed to fly north almost out of sight in between targets.

0530-SUNRISE

Shortly before daybreak, the NVA forces executed an all-out assault on the district headquarters. Just before dawn, they attacked with human wave attacks on all sides except the southern and part of the eastern perimeters, making all manner of noises from the south and southwest, and launching strong attacks again against the western and northwestern perimeter. Some of the noise sounded like metal on metal. For a brief period, bugles sounded as if to say "charge!" Their effort from the north was just enough to cause our diminishing number of healthy soldiers to be spread even more thinly around the entire perimeter. This was by far their strongest attack—their "do or die" effort. Those of us inside the compound could sense this and knew we had to hold the compound or die. In a few words, the potential outcome of this attack was absolutely terrifying!

Had we not been through the previous 24 hours of alternating periods of terror, then position consolidation and recovery, then again thinking, *This is it, we are going to die*, we may have withered on the vine with this attack. But most of us now believed that we could out-think and out-fight them during this attack. At that point, I had an inkling or sense of what the term "battle-hardened" might mean. We were afraid but no longer too terrified to fight. It was amazing to see the courage and determination of the South Vietnamese soldiers. Only hours earlier, they had considered trying to escape our compound or surrender. Now they were performing like hardened combat soldiers. That, in and of itself, was a miracle. And seeing them certainly encouraged me as well.

As the NVA approached, we could see that they were using civilians as hostages to shield them. There were *so* many of them. It was difficult to comprehend that this was really happening. They began to breach the western perimeter, and I requested ARVN artillery low airbursts on the western perimeter. Then I ran around the perimeter to warn my soldiers that I had called in an artillery airburst. This time, the ARVN sought overhead cover much faster than they had the previous night. I warned the FACs to stay clear of the north of my western compound. Friendly artillery was firing south from their northern position. I told the FACs that they should adjust their flight pattern accordingly, and they did.

Many refugees had been forced to occupy and surround the schoolhouse near my northwest perimeter. I believed they were there to prevent us from shooting the NVA when they attacked across the open area. Some were used as human shields. Some NVA troops carried wood planks to place on the barbed wire as they breached the perimeter. In some cases, I was told the NVA walked on civilians as they breached the perimeter. I was later told that some of the civilians were dead, some wounded, some neither.

With civilians being used as shields, we were hesitant to fire at them, thereby allowing the NVA soldiers to access our perimeter. I ran to the top level of the tower with my constant companion, the good marksman, and several others he recruited, and we were able to shoot over the heads of the civilians and hit the attacking NVA soldiers. Doing that likely went a long way to slowing the attack and reducing the number of enemies who actually breached our perimeter. In talking with the FACs weeks later, they thought we had a machine gun in the tower.

No, it was my sharpshooter and me, with three others reloading our M16s.

When I left to communicate with the FACs or return to the perimeter, my sharpshooter and his loaders stayed the course in the tower.

People were running everywhere outside our west and northwest perimeters. It seemed to be a mix of civilians, Viet Cong clothed in black, and NVA soldiers in their battle uniforms. So many were trying to get to and into our perimeter, and a large number were trying to run anywhere *except* toward our perimeter. It was quite obvious that we were losing this battle, if for no other reason than being grossly outnumbered. You can only shoot and reload so fast, which, in numerous cases, was not fast enough. Thus, hand-to-hand fighting ensued. All our walking wounded were told to stay on the perimeter, and most did.

Capt. Nguyen and I were running around the perimeter, encouraging our soldiers while placing our soldiers, weapons, and ammunition wherever needed to combat the constantly changing situation. The situation was critical. I told the FACs we needed their flechettes on our perimeter. They seemed a little reluctant to provide this at first. They could see what was happening on the ground, yet you had to be on the ground to really appreciate the gravity of the situation. Soon, they were convinced that I needed to place anything they had on the western perimeter. Flechettes, rockets, cluster bombs, and tactical air all had my approval. Without some of these weapons deployed on and near our perimeter almost immediately, we were doomed.

The noise level was extremely high. I would be in the upper level of the tower, then back down, running around the perimeter and repositioning my soldiers, returning fire on the berm, and then back up in the tower. I did this back and forth from tower to perimeter for what seemed to be hours. In reality, it was probably no more than about two hours.

ON OR ABOUT 0615 HOURS

Additional excerpts are provided from Capt. Personett's "Point of the Spear" article:

The first rays of sunlight appear on the horizon. The last stage of the battle starts. NVA bugles sound and the first wave of NVA come out of the schoolhouse and approach the west wall for the compound firing their AK-47s. The defenders cannot respond except for one man. He is located at the top of a 25-foot concrete tower in the middle of the compound. He has an M-60 with him and is continuously firing at the advancing troops. Because of his height advantage he is able to shoot over the heads of the refugees and into the NVA. The other ARVN soldiers, now waiting behind the compound wall for the advancing NVA troops, cannot shoot for fear of hitting the refugees. I am sure they are the only ones more frustrated than we are this morning. Several of the refugees fall, either shot or tripped by the tangle wire. The compound wall erupts with withering fire. The NVA start to go down. The refugees panic and run into the ensuing crossfire. It quickly turns into a killing field. It is madness.

The second NVA assault was lining up again behind the refugees while the mortars continued to fall. This time it was more of a charge than the last time. It was a desperate attempt to get across the free fire zone before the ARVN come out of their bunkers. It almost worked except for the ARVN M-60 gunner in the tower. As soon as the refugees and the NVA hit the berm at the base of the west wall the NVA were once again exposed to the M-60 fire. It chewed the NVA forces up. The mortars continued. The NVA starting firing RPGs from the corner of the schoolhouse toward the tower. It took two direct hits, but it did not go down.

Several waves of NVA were attempted against the west wall. Had they instead used some of their west wall forces against our south and east perimeters, we most likely would have been completely overrun. There were lulls between west perimeter attacks.

After the second attack, the lulls were getting longer in duration. I kept hoping they were giving up and would go away.

The FACs, Covey 111 and Covey 100, were absolutely fabulous and courageous with their response. They began flying incredibly low, attacking my perimeter. They made nine or more passes, firing everything they had. I was in the upper tower watching them attack our western perimeter. Even in Hollywood movies, I had never seen aircraft attack a ground installation by dropping their ordnance merely several yards above the target. I was simply awestruck. They were taking anti-aircraft machine gun-type fire with each pass. I warned them of this and told them not to come in so close. I was amazed that no harm had come to them.

WOW! Hallelujah! There was another Covey in the air. He arrived to relieve Coveys 100 and 111 and was communicating with them, not me. He had taken over adjusting the Naval gunfire as well, while A-7 Corsairs launched from an aircraft carrier in the South China Sea. The A-7s were providing close air support bombing while Coveys 111 and 100 were supporting me against the ground assaults. The U.S. assets of the Air Force, Marines, Navy, and Army were putting a hurt on the mortar and artillery positions of the 2nd NVA Division. This battle had become a well-coordinated joint-service operation. From my vantage point, I was ecstatic, relieved, and beginning to see a path for survival.

Were my thoughts somewhat premature?

Excerpts from the "Point of the Spear" article continue:

There was a lull in the fighting. I asked Rich if he was OK. Either our ordnance was gone, or we were shot up so badly we could not fire any. Our fuel was going fast. We probably had more than one hole in more than one tank. Otherwise, we were OK. I could hardly hear Rich on the intercom for all the air noise caused by the air rushing through our bullet-hole filled cockpit. I thought it is time to go home, Rich. The fighting has stopped. We can still make Quang Ngai if we go now.

Then that voice from the ARVN compound, that desperate and yet determined voice, that has always been so full of resolve, that voice I have come to know so well over the last seven hours, speaks once again to us for the last time. It tells us that the NVA are massing for a final assault. He wants us to use everything we have to stop them. It is OK for us to direct the A-7s to drop the MK-82 bombs on his position. He tells us this is it. We are not going to give up and we are not going to order his destruction. We do not tell them we have nothing left to shoot ourselves. Now what? Fight or flight? The early morning sun's rays light us up quite nicely. We have lost our invisibility. Our cloak of darkness is gone. The .50 cal AAA guns are really trying to get us now.

Joe?

Yes!

Down we go as the next human wave assault comes hurling at the compound wall. We have just as much chance of stopping it as we would a real wave on that nearby beautiful beach I saw before we rolled in. What did we roll in for? This is not a strafing or rocket pass. It is to fake them into thinking it is one. They do not fake out. I tell Rich to drop the LAU pods on the next pass and he does. Now we are bowling for NVA with LAU pods.

Get Lower.

The .50 cal guns can only deflect so low, and we try to stay below them. WE ARE REALLY LOW.

Suddenly there is blood in the cockpit.

Have I been hit? No.

Rich? I shake the stick. He is OK.

Whose blood is it? Then it dawns on me that enemy blood is coming off the propeller tips through the bullet holes in the cockpit backseat and onto my face and lap.

We probably have time for one more run and then that is it. We are going to make 'silk letdowns' if we do not leave. We see the NVA standing outside the compound fence firing into the compound. On this, our last pass, we use our left-wing tip to give the NVA a lesson in wing tip vortices. We are now done and headed home. I remember the wide, high, left climbing turn toward the southeast as we pull off the target. Right at the top of the pull out the left engine sputters and quits and we start to roll left. I instinctively grab the stick and apply top rudder. The stick is mush in my hands. It is not connected to anything. We roll inverted and now start to spin.

The FACs were doing such a great job that I had stopped watching them and returned to the perimeter as an individual reinforcement. Then, someone yelled that the airplane had crashed.

Impossible. I just saw it go dangerously low in front of me and climb up, heading sort of south.

Several others were nodding their heads, indicating the opposite. I raced back to and up the tower. First, I saw smoke and then the plane and then maybe a parachute on the ground. *Maybe one of them got out.* No one was visible. But that was just wishful thinking on my part. What a sinking feeling. The two aviators whom I credited with saving my life were now dead. They had been flying this critical support mission for seven to eight hours.

The plane had crashed on the east side of Dong Cat near an area with many palm trees. This was an area previously reported to be held by an estimated NVA battalion and was about 300 yards from my location. This was not good, but the pilots had probably died in the crash anyway. I immediately reported the shoot down to my headquarters and then requested ARVN fire near that location. Unfortunately, I was told it was out of their range. Within what seemed to be a short period of time, an Army helicopter arrived. I first saw it in the area of the crashed OV-10. It was smaller than a Huey helicopter, probably a light observation helicopter. It dropped from my sight below the tree line and then reappeared with someone half in and half out of the helicopter. I was overjoyed. At least one of the U.S. Air Force (USAF) pilots had survived. Then, suddenly, the helicopter dropped out of sight. My heart sank. Two pilots that most likely saved me and my Vietnamese soldiers from being overrun were dead. And now, one or two Army pilots were probably dead as well.

Capt. Joe Personett and Capt. Rich Poling had ejected safely from their OV-10. Joe had watched Rich's descent and landing.

Here are a few more excerpts from Captain Personett's "Point of the Spear":

I was now submerged on my stomach, up to my neck in the water, frantically trying to find my radio while apprehensively looking at the tree line where I expected to see the NVA charging toward me. For some unknown reason they were not coming out of the trees to kill Rich or me. Why not, I thought? Rich was halfway between me and the tree line. The water I was in was about 18 inches deep and the rice was about six inches above the water line. It was now very peaceful and quiet except for the bees that I kept hearing that were buzzing around my head. 'How can I hear with my acoustic flight helmet on, I thought?' I took my helmet off and instantly realized that the bees were really bullets passing through the rice next to my head...

Just then I heard a chopper off to my right rear coming into a hover near Rich. Rich had gotten his radio working right away. He had contacted the A-7s circling overhead. They then put out a call on guard for any chopper in the area to come and pick up two downed pilots. The first chopper to respond to that call was based near Quang Ngai. They did not hesitate to answer the call alone. The chopper was an Army LOH or 'Loach' with a crew of two armed with a minigun. I watched in fascination as the Loach came to a hover over Rich's chute and then turned quickly to the left 180 degrees, then back to the right 360 degrees, then back to the left again. They were looking for Rich but they could not find him, because they were turning so fast they kept missing sight of him There he is! He is standing up now so they will see him. What balls to stand up in front of the tree line! The Loach sees him and is coming in next to him. He was getting in the chopper. They have got him!

*The tree line erupts with everything the NVA had. The .50 Cal
they moved into place was waiting for this moment. The little Loach
was chewed up like it was made of cardboard. It just stopped flying and
dropped like a rock. Three bodies came flying out even before the impact
waves had started to spread across the rice paddy. I am stunned and
instantly depressed. I rolled onto my back with just my nose sticking out
of the water. Rich and the Loach pilots are surely dead. No one could have
survived that many rounds going into their machine.*

Only a single FAC remained in the air, and he was not paying
much attention to my situation. In fact, he was directing the A-7
Corsairs as they dropped bombs on and around the tree line near
the downed OV-10. He had arrived on station about 20-30 minutes
earlier. I later learned that the concussion from their bombs had
caused the ceiling of a nearby house used by an NVA battalion staff
to collapse, allegedly killing the battalion commander and some of
his staff.

Two army gunships arrived and began firing into the tree line.
Now another Army Huey helicopter was circling several hundred
yards north of the downed OV-10. Where had all these helicopters
and their firepower been earlier when I needed them and probably
still did? But no one was talking to me at this time.

So much was going on in the air and on the ground. All I could
do was watch some of the activity—and some of it wasn't even visible from my location! Up until the shootdown, the battle had been
raging and we were barely holding our own. It seemed that the tide
changed almost instantaneously with the arrival of our helicopters
and close air support jet aircraft. The NVA must have realized they
had the short end of the stick and retreated back into the refugee
camp and hamlets, at least for the moment.

Several hours later, I was told that Army helicopters rescued
both Captains Poling and Personett and the Army pilots. Captain
Poling was the man that I had seen hanging half in half out of the
Loach helicopter.

Captain Personett's rescue experience was similarly interesting and just as breathtaking as that of Captain Poling's. Here are more excerpts from Captain Personett's "Point of the Spear" article:

I looked to my left toward the now smoldering Loach and see one, no two Cobra helicopters gunships working the tree line. I look around me and now see there are a total of four of them. One of them just passes over me. I see a Huey 200 yards away just above the tree line. The Huey turns towards me. I think they see me. I get up and start moving toward him. I feel like I am trying to run in quicksand. I am smiling as I run toward the chopper. Then I see water splashing near me. It is splashing in lines toward the Huey. The Huey is being hosed down from somewhere behind me. Hell, I am being hosed. The door gunner is aiming right at me. I know that the tracers from his gun are aimed at my head. No, they are going over my head to somewhere behind me. The Huey is continuing to sparkle as bullets hit it, yet it stays in the hover. The chopper is going to be shot down and I am going to die, just like Rich. It is time to 'stand and deliver.'

I stop running and try turning quickly to my right with my .38 in my right hand. I stop turning with my back to the Huey. I see before me the three NVA who had been tracking me earlier. They were standing in the rice paddy 10 yards behind me. They were standing line abreast, five feet apart, shooting at the Huey. I was between them and the Huey. They had their AK-47s on full automatic. I had a six shot .38. I pulled the trigger before I aimed. The first NVA on the left was already doubling up and going down as I tried to sight in on him. He looked like he had been sawed in half. I pulled the trigger again and again. I switched to the next man in line. I started to sight in on him as his head exploded like a ripe watermelon after being shot with shotgun. I kept pulling the trigger. I looked in fear at the last NVA standing on the right as he went over backwards with his finger still on the trigger while his AK-47 was sending out its' last rounds, now arching up into the sky. I thought I am going to be killed by a dead man, just as his last rounds went by me and into the chopper. Just then my legs crumpled.

I felt like I had been hit behind the knees by a baseball bat. It was the skid of the Huey hitting the back of my legs. The Huey had moved up behind me while the gunfight was going on. I was still looking in amazement at the three dead NVA when the Huey hit me. Sergeant Justin, the door gunner, had just killed these three NVA without killing me in the process. Justin had grabbed the back of my flight suit as I was falling backwards onto the skid. He pulled me inside the Huey with his right arm as he continuously fired the M-60 with his left hand. The Huey crew had held their ground and because of that had just saved my life. They stood and delivered.

I was now on my back on the floor of the Huey as it lifted off. I sat up and got my plastic bag out that held my extra ammo. I unlocked the cylinder to eject the shell casings and reload. Bullets, not shell casings came out into my hand. Not one round had fired from my gun. It was around eleven a.m. now. My gun and bullets had been underwater for more than three hours and not one bullet had fired. I was shocked. I stood up and looked down at my gun in one hand and my bullets in the other.

Let me get this straight here and now: Capt. Poling had switched places with Capt. Personett during the refuel rearm trip back to Da Nang and was the pilot of a USAF OV-10 Bronco when shot down over Mo Duc sometime between 0700 to 0800 hours on September 17. After about an hour, he was rescued by a U.S. Army Loach, only to be shot down in this aircraft during the rescue attempt. An hour or two after that, a second rescue attempt was made by a U.S. Army Huey. This attempt was successful. Capt. Poling was shot down twice in a 60-90-minute period while in aircraft of two different military services. He certainly had a lucky charm somewhere on his body. With the rescue of all the downed pilots, the overall battlefield was quieter and more peaceful for a few hours.

During the next hour or so, Capt. Nguyen and I counted dead NVA soldiers in or near our perimeter. I stopped counting at 200. He reported the final count as 265. A number of them were wearing sashes that read "Liberate Mo Duc or Die" and "To Sacrifice for One's Country, Liberate Mo Duc." We spent the remainder of the morning tending to our wounded, repairing concertina wire, and doing myriad things to prepare for another assault. It remained quiet until early afternoon.

1300–2400 HOURS

Off and on during the battle, a machine gun in Dong Cat hamlet fired into our compound. The gunner had a good view into the compound through the main gate and would cut loose with a long burst when he saw one of us walking in the compound.

He also enjoyed shooting at the tower, probably out of boredom or just because it was there. Either way, I did not appreciate it. It was a nuisance, to say the least.

My soldiers thought they neutralized him several times during the afternoon, but he seemed to remain at his position until we thought we had shot him. Eventually, the machine gunner stopped firing altogether. Other snipers surrounding us were active during the afternoon and after dark. Mortars continued firing at us periodically, primarily as interdiction and harassing fires, or so I believed. They just wanted to keep us on edge and let us know they were still hanging around. We were delighted that nothing more was occurring.

Even the U.S. Air Force and Navy realized the battlefield had simmered down considerably. At first, I was uneasy about their departure. But the weather had greatly improved, and I knew their support was readily available again if needed. Still, the possibility of another attack was extremely concerning. The village and hamlet radios reported significant troop concentrations and artillery behind the southern end of LZ Dragon. That area was still under NVA control. They also reported NVA losses had been significant over the previous 24 hours.

Our small arms ammunition was almost depleted, and we did not have enough ammo to last more than a brief time if we were attacked again. Without a secure means of communication, I was hesitant to reveal this problem, without encryption, to my higher headquarters. Besides, they did not have a reasonably safe capability to resupply us.

The civilian radios were fairly quiet at this point, and the villagers were not reporting targets. The captain and I were not sure why. We decided that the village elders knew of targets, but the mortar and artillery positions were not preparing for action. Sometimes, it is better to let a sleeping dog lie. *Maybe both sides had had enough action for a while.*

At some point in the evening, we learned that Highway 1 entering Mo Duc from Tu Nghia district in the north and Highway 1 south of Duc My Village near the Duc Pho District to the south had NVA blocking forces in place for several days. Attempts by ARVN forces from Tu Ngai to come to Mo Duc's aid had been unsuccessful so far. I was incredibly pleased that I had made Staff Sgt. Bassinett return to Quang Ngai City on the evening of September 15. We most definitely needed his assistance during the battle and with the wounded. However, in all probability, he would have been killed or captured by the NVA's northern blocking force had he not returned to province HQ.

Capt. Nguyen was excited. He had just received information that elements of the 2nd ARVN Division had been flown to locations several miles north of us and were attempting to fight their way into our headquarters. I was also excited but quickly said I hoped they got there before we ran out of ammo. He knew the ammo situation better than me, and we were in good shape with our mortar ammo on hand. Our small arms ammo was now even less than reported several hours prior that morning. Capt. Nguyen's excitement turned to concern. He knew the ARVN soldiers would not be able to get here until the following day. We had to survive the night.

Around 2300 hours, I discussed the concept of harassment and interdiction (H&I) fires we employed with our artillery in the 1st Cavalry Division with Capt. Nguyen. He already understood the use of H&I fires using light artillery. I suggested we do the same thing with our small arms and mortar fire.

By having small arms fire from different locations during the night and early morning, it would somewhat bother the NVA. But it could let them believe we were not worried about running out of ammunition. My suggestion was not well received at first. I continued saying that if we were attacked at that time, we would be out of ammo in 15 minutes. But it was worth taking a chance. He eventually agreed and implemented these H&I fires. The small arms H&I fires were, shall we say, infrequent but provided nonetheless.

The NVA implemented their own H&I fires against us throughout the night. No one slept much on either side. Most of us did not sleep that night for fear of another assault. It was Sunday evening, and I had not eaten much since Friday. I accepted a small bowl of hot rice someone handed me, and the adrenaline was still flowing in me and in most of us.

Crater holes inside Maj. Collier's Mo Duc district perimeter following the battle, September 1972. Photo provided by Col. Bill Collier.

CHAPTER TEN
THE BATTLE FOR MO DUC, THIRD DAY

18 SEPTEMBER 1972, MONDAY
0530–0800 HOURS

After a sleepless night full of anticipation, listening to the sounds of war a short distance away and receiving only periodic sniper fire during the early hours, everyone was on the perimeter waiting for an early morning assault. The ammo count revealed less than 300 rounds total remaining for our M-16 rifles.

Capt. Nguyen told me reports from the refugee camp—and even Dong Cat—indicated that the NVA were slowly backing out of those areas. Reports from units further south and north showed no change. They were still under NVA control. What were we to believe? Was the siege of the Mo Duc district headquarters over? Could I really let myself believe that I had survived? My wishful thinking may have been a bit premature. My Vietnamese team members were more concerned about their families' status and well-being than the fact that we were about to be attacked. They were still looking to me for direction. An attack did not appear to be imminent, and worry for the wounded and dying soldiers, as well as wanting to gain information about their families, seemed to be their overriding concerns now. In dealing with both concerns, I was out of my comfort zone.

0800–1100 HOURS

Two inbound Huey helicopters landed just outside the district head-quarters. Approximately seven or eight ARVN soldiers exited each chopper and entered the compound. Capt. Nguyen said they were with the 2nd ARVN Division that had been fighting its way to us since the previous day. Their purpose was to relieve our district soldiers on the perimeter and secure the district headquarters. They appeared to be startled at what they saw: A friendly armored unit was enroute to this location from the north. I mentally decided that the battle for Mo Duc headquarters was probably over. It had been 54 hours since hostilities began. My Vietnamese soldiers sensed my belief, too.

I did not think I could contain them inside the compound much longer. It was time to find out about their families. Capt. Nguyen and I divided most of our healthy and some of the mobile, lightly wounded soldiers into groups based on where they lived. There were six groups of five or less soldiers, and most groups had fewer than five. Only two groups were allowed to leave the compound at a time. The groups had to carry their loaded weapons, keep each other in sight at all times, check on the well-being of their families, and quickly return so the next two groups could depart.

I went with the first group. Sergeant First Class (SFC) Long elected to go with me instead of a later group that would go in the vicinity of his family's location. I knew he was anxious about his family, yet he was extremely loyal in his job with the Americans.

As we departed the district headquarters, our initial interest was the buildings where the persistent machine gunner(s) had fired on us. The villagers eagerly showed us the cone-shaped wood stake with a large, thick rope attached to it and the other end attached around the ankles of NVA machine gunners. This was that irritating machine gun position Sammy, others, and I thought we had neutralized several times yesterday. From what I learned, when one NVA gunner was wounded or killed, another was tied there in his place. They were unable to seek sufficient cover when my soldiers took aim at them. I saw one of the uniformed NVA who had been tied to the stake—he appeared to be young. The villagers said most of them were 17 years old or younger. The machine gun they were firing still had some packing grease on it, indicating that it was new or had only recently been used, probably initially for this battle. The ammunition for it was abundant.

We were shown several red capsules taken off NVA bodies. The capsules contained a white powder that the villagers said was a narcotic. Each soldier also carried enough food for an estimated 14 days.

I asked Capt. Nguyen for a friendly body count and was informed that 99 out of 120 of his ARVN force had been killed or wounded. Most of our casualties were wounded rather than killed. The NVA dragged a large number of their dead and wounded off the battlefield. Therefore, their actual body count was unknown, but it had to be in the high hundreds. The total number of NVA estimated dead during the three-day siege was between 400-500. This included kills by the U.S. Air Force and Navy, ARVN artillery, as well as us as the defenders of the district headquarters. It also included numbers received from village and hamlet elders based on their sightings as the NVA quickly recovered and removed their wounded and dead from the battle area.

1100–1700 HOURS

Five armored personnel carriers (APCs) arrived, each with a complement of soldiers inside. They were an ARVN Ranger group supporting the 2nd ARVN Division. Apparently, they had just swept through some of the areas near the district headquarters.

Throughout the battle, SFC Long had worried that the NVA would find out about his family living in Dong Cat or, even worse, perhaps his family had been hurt during some of the fighting in that hamlet. One of the APC Rangers approached SFC Long and handed him something. As it turned out, his wife had sent a bowl of Chinese soup for him, which was her way of telling him that his family was OK. He fell to his knees, having an emotional moment. SFC Long had not shown any fear or other emotion during the battle. Most of the time, he stayed with me, except when I asked him to distribute ammo or relay orders to Capt. Nguyen from time to time. Yes, the Vietnamese are incredible human beings.

We spent several hours putting out fires, looking after the wounded, and trying to clear a lot of debris. The Ranger medic began treating our wounded with the limited medical supplies he had. Capt. Nguyen and the Ranger captain approached me to say that unless we could get a number of our wounded to a hospital, they would soon die. I needed to evacuate Staff Sgt. Jackson to Quang Ngai City as soon as possible. After some discussion, it was decided that I would take the seriously wounded, a few non-local ARVN dead, and Jackson and Sandy (my KIA interpreter) to Quang Ngai City. I believed that ensuring Jackson's travel and delivery to American authorities in Quang Ngai City was my task to do.

A captured NVA flag and sash worn by NVA soldiers attacking Mo Duc. These items were seized from the enemy on September 17, 1972.

1700–2400 HOURS

Three APCs were needed. Staff Sgt. Jackson and the Vietnamese KIA were placed in one. The seriously wounded were placed in the other two APCs. The lightly wounded—that is, those thought not to have life-threatening wounds—were to remain at Mo Duc. The Ranger captain showed me his intended route north to Tu Nghia. He said it was too dangerous to take Highway 1, which would have been the most direct and fastest route. I agreed with him. We would go east, cross the Thoa River tributary, turn north, and work our way northeast to the village of Duc Tho, enter Highway 1, and cross the bridge into Tu Nghia district. I was familiar with most of the planned route. The captain said that the NVA was mostly on the west side of Highway 1. Until we got near Duc Tho, we would be traveling east of Highway 1. The trip should take about three hours.

Only the wounded, dead, and APC drivers would be inside the APCs. Each APC had a machine gun with a gunner and four riflemen riding on top. The Ranger captain rode on top of the lead APC, I rode on top of the middle APC, and a Ranger sergeant rode on top of the third APC.

We departed out the main gate, turned north on Highway 1 for a quarter of a mile, then turned east-northeast until we reached the Thoa River tributary. Much to our dismay, the heretofore narrow tributary was quite wide, having overflowed its banks during the typhoon. The APCs had to be prepared to swim the river.

This would be a new experience for me.

The preparation took at least 30 minutes as we sat there in an open rice paddy. That 30 minutes seemed more like 3 hours, and I was incredibly anxious during that time. Finally, they were ready to "swim" the river. Upon entering the water, we found that the current was too strong. Control of the APCs for direction was limited, and it took a mile or more to get to the other side. What should have been a 10-minute river crossing for all three APCs was more like an hour. During the downstream swim, at one time or another, each APC came to the shore on the wrong side and/or got stuck somewhere. We were now in an area south of Mo Duc where elements of the 3rd NVA Division were reported to be a blocking force against Duc Pho, the district directly south of Mo Duc district. My pucker factor was rapidly rising once again. This river crossing suddenly had all the makings of a disaster. When we departed Mo Duc HQ, I was concerned that it would get dark before we arrived near the Tu Nghia border. Now, with the delays resulting from the less than textbook river-crossing, I was also concerned that we would be discovered by the bad guys before it got dark.

The Ranger captain showed me how he intended to get back to his original route and told us to be quiet so that the NVA would not hear us. *Quiet?* APCs are not as loud as tanks, but they are definitely and distinctly loud. In any case, we were now moving toward our original travel route.

It was almost dark. There was absolutely no electricity in this part of Vietnam. The skies were only partly cloudy, and the stars were shining brightly. It was a beautiful night, and we were moving slowly. After another hour or so, we pulled into a tree line. The captain had been told that NVA might be in the area, so we sat there for several hours, engines off. We could see flares and artillery being fired in the vicinity of Mo Duc. After a while, I realized that the targets were west of Mo Duc and most likely being fired at the NVA. *That* was a good feeling. The Ranger captain talked periodically with someone on his tactical radio. My mind was playing different scenarios of what should or could be our next course of action to get to the Tu Nghia bridge. There did not seem to be many safe and easy options.

CHAPTER ELEVEN
THE BATTLE FOR MO DUC, FOURTH DAY

19 SEPTEMBER 1972, TUESDAY
MIDNIGHT–0600 HOURS

Lying on my back on top of the APC, looking up at the stars, was surreal. Other than the distant occasional artillery sounds and flashes, the countryside was very quiet. With palm trees all around me, everything was beautiful and peaceful. Even my nostrils considered the pungent smells—especially from the rice paddies just a few yards away—as normal, giving me a safe and comfortable feeling. In the space of a few minutes, I saw two different aircraft flying over Vietnam, both going eastward. They were high in the night sky, probably passenger planes flying at an altitude of 35,000 feet, going in the direction of the U.S. I thought about how wonderful it would be if I were on one of them.

I would love to be home with my family right now.

My nostalgia for family and everything in America was suddenly interrupted by the noise of a single-engine propeller-driven airplane. His altitude couldn't have been more than 2,000 to 2,500 feet. Over my radio, I heard him calling, "Mike 36."

Hey! That's me!

But I did not want to answer him for fear of revealing my position. The small airplane kept crisscrossing the district from Highway 1 to the South China Sea and back again. By the fifth or sixth time I heard him call "Mike 36," I just had to answer. After all, no other American in this whole wide world knew my approximate location other than the pilot in that airplane. I had thoughts that if I were killed now, no one would know where to find my body. I keyed my radio and, in a whisper, answered him.

He asked for my location. I had no intention of providing my grid coordinates in the clear for anyone listening to hear, and I told him so. Besides, our three-APC convoy was about halfway between Highway 1 and the coast. This area was flat, alternating with small hamlets and rice paddies. To someone unfamiliar with this area, it all looked the same. Determining reasonably accurate coordinates would require using a flashlight, possibly revealing our location. I asked him to make all further communications in a whisper. He insisted that he wanted a better "fix" on my location than what he was guessing at that point. I had a strobe light and said I would give him two flashes, but only when he was ready. A few minutes later, he gave me the go-ahead. After my two flashes, he indicated he knew my location and would blink his running lights when he was directly over my location.

As his running lights blinked directly over me, I felt a hint of joy. What a great feeling! At least one American knew where I was. For the moment, I relaxed and felt somewhat comfortable and secure, which was, of course, ridiculous. He could only know *approximately* where I was.

Well, that was better than nothing… Maybe.

0200 HOURS
AMBUSH

The Ranger captain came over to me and said, "We go." The APC engines started. We were on our way again. Realistically, I had no choice but to leave the route management and my personal safety to the Ranger captain.

After about two hours of slowly moving west-northwest, we drove up to Highway 1. That area looked familiar. I believed we were only a few miles from the bridge over the Ve River and safety. The bridge was on Highway 1. It was a single-lane wooden bridge that had been destroyed and rebuilt numerous times during the past eight or nine years. The river was some 30-40 feet below. Placed on top of the wood bridge frame were two thick planks, each about two feet wide, for vehicular traffic to line up their wheels on to cross.

We were getting close to the bridge. The surroundings were familiar to me as we approached a hamlet. Suddenly, several civilians appeared and motioned for the convoy to pull over near the edge of the hamlet. The Ranger captain dismounted his APC to talk with these local civilians, after which he came back to brief me on his discussions. I had noticed during the stop that all the soldiers on each APC were fully alert and ready to fire their weapons.

The civilians warned the Ranger captain that an ambush was being prepared for his convoy immediately before the bridge.

Will I ever get to safety? I wondered.

The Ranger captain was concerned. Actually, he seemed perplexed. He had lost the image of confidence he had displayed up until that point. Sensing this, I thought it was time to help him think through this situation. To be frank, his loss of confidence had not helped my confidence any. He had learned we had unknowingly passed through several of the locations where the NVA blocking force had been until the 2nd ARVN division dislodged them yesterday. *Wow!* Now ahead of us were local Viet Cong and a few NVA stragglers, which really did pose a serious problem. To make matters worse, I had left SFC Long in the Mo Duc district headquarters. The Ranger captain had worked with American advisors before, but his advisor and interpreter were in Tu Nghia.

Oh boy! It was going to be interesting to develop a new plan with people whom I had not worked with previously, and no one had their interpreter with them. The Ranger captain used his limited ability to speak English, and I used my limited ability to speak

Vietnamese. Together, we somehow managed to agree on certain considerations and a course of action. To backtrack now, especially in the dark, was too dangerous. And the bad guys knew who we were and where we were. To remain in this hamlet was also dangerous, as the local VC had identified themselves and were willing to attack us. Of course, to go west where the bulk of the NVA remained was out of the question. To go forward was to possibly enter an ambush.

Well, maybe the ambush was not fully prepared. My mission was to get Staff Sgt. Jackson and the wounded Vietnamese to a hospital. I could see no other choice but to run the ambush and hope it had not been fully established. It was not quite dawn, and our presence was probably only recently made known to them. The Ranger captain agreed with me to run the ambush.

The plan was to keep the same convoy order of march. If the Ranger captain's APC became disabled or stalled while crossing the bridge, my APC was to push his off the bridge. If my APC became disabled or stalled on the bridge, the third APC was to push my APC off the bridge. The Ranger captain, a Ranger sergeant, three APC drivers, and I discussed these instructions until I felt they understood and seemed willing to comply. I said, "OK, let's do it." To my surprise, everyone started hugging one another. That was when I *knew* they understood.

We started down Highway 1 at a fairly rapid pace. Maybe five minutes down the road and about a hundred yards from the bridge, all hell broke loose. Bullets were hitting the sides of the APCs and making an awful racket. Those of us on top of the APCs were hugging the top with all our strength. My machine gunner was wildly spraying the area. It was like a "mad minute" from the 1st Cavalry Division days, except I was on the receiving end this time. We ran the static ambush in about a minute, more or less. Several rocket-propelled grenades (RPGs) were fired at us with only one nipping the third APC. It kept going, and we made it across the bridge. To this day, I believe the VC/NVA were not completely ready for us when we rolled through their ambush. Ready or not, it was scary as hell… and somewhat fun at the same time!

Some of the command staff of the ARVN Ranger group were on the other side of the river waiting for us. My APC stopped on a slight incline. When I jumped off the APC, I tumbled to the ground and lost my steel helmet. Someone walked over to me, handed my helmet to me, and in perfect English said, "Welcome to Tu Nghia, Major." I looked up to see an American major named Major Martin. I thanked him and added that he was the best-looking person I had seen in days. He replied, "I can understand that." I never saw Maj. Martin again. Looking back, there are many Americans from those times I would cherish seeing again.

ARRIVAL IN QUANG NGAI CITY
0430-0500 HOURS

Our APC convoy safely moved through the district of Tu Nghia and arrived in Quang Ngai City shortly after dawn. My boss, Col. Truman Bowman, was still in bed when I banged hard on his door. When he opened the door and saw me, he gave me a big bear hug. He was a stoutly built infantryman, and I thought he was going to crush my chest. After a short conversation during which he made some nice comments, he showed me a room where I could sleep and then have some breakfast in their mess hall when I was ready. He said we could talk more in his office after breakfast.

It was now September 19, and I had not slept since awakening the morning of September 16. After lying in bed for two hours staring at the ceiling and thinking, I got up and went to the mess hall, which, I think, was actually an enlarged kitchen.

CHAPTER TWELVE
BRIEFINGS AND BANQUET

19 SEPTEMBER 1972 (CONTINUED)
0530 HOURS

After seeing Col. Bowman and being told to go sleep, eat breakfast, and come to his office, I entered the "mess facility" shortly before 0600 hours, where an assortment of people were also just arriving for their breakfast. Vietnamese cooks, trained to prepare meals that Americans typically enjoyed, were present in the kitchen. Frankly, I had no idea who owned, controlled, or operated this facility. What I did know is that the province advisory team acted as if they were in charge. However, this was my first time entering this facility.

The early morning patrons I could identify included Air America pilots, suspected CIA operations officers, American province advisors, Vietnamese who were employed by the MACV Province Advisory Team 17, and another group of five Americans who were not very friendly or outgoing. The aroma of coffee filled the air, making the room warm and inviting. Most people smiled, nodded, or said, "Good morning," and then continued on with their coffee or food. No one had any idea who I was or what I had just been through. It was as if I was living a dream. My last meal was dinner on September 15, though I did have a small bowl of rice the day before. Even as hungry as I was, for some strange reason, I did not want to eat at first. Finally, I ate some scrambled eggs with toast. It was delicious. After eating, I went to Col. Bowman's office to await his arrival.

The MACV Province Advisory Team 17 headquarters was located in a nice, large, permanent structure, probably built and used by high-ranking French personnel in the 1940s or early 1950s. The province-level Advisory Team 17 had been working on living facilities that far exceeded those of the district-level advisors. In fact, these advisors lived much better than district advisors on several levels!

BRIEFING TO COLONEL TRUMAN BOWMAN, THE QUANG NGAI PROVINCE SENIOR ADVISOR: 0800 HOURS

During the next hour or more, Col. Bowman and I discussed many aspects concerning the battle. He seemed satisfied with our discussions about this seemingly insignificant battle. In reality, the battle for Mo Duc involved all U.S. military services except the U.S. Coast Guard and prevented an NVA infantry division from conquering the entire district of Mo Duc. To me, it was a great example of our combined military services successfully working together on the battlefield.

It was during our discussions that we both realized the significance of the battle for Mo Duc. Throughout the battle, half of my six-member district advisor team had been killed. A fourth member, Sammy, had been seriously wounded. The district operations officer said that approximately 99 of the 120 soldiers inside the district headquarters had been killed or wounded. Thankfully, most were only wounded. Two American aircraft had been shot down: An OV-10 Bronco and an Army Loach lay crumpled in the rice paddies around Mo Duc.

At one point, and at the same time, two U.S. Air Force (USAF) pilots and two U.S. Army aviators were on the ground in different locations near enemy positions, hoping for and awaiting rescue.

The USS Hanson and a second American naval vessel provided fire support that absolutely contributed to the successful defense of our position. Cumulative NVA and Viet Cong KIAs were probably as high as 800 or more throughout Mo Duc district. Navy Corsair A-7 aircraft launched from an American aircraft carrier in the South China Sea and F-4 aircraft launched from Ubon, Thailand, provided tactical air support, which was critical to the battle. After the aviators were shot down and the skies were now clear, at least one USAF FAC and numerous Army helicopters arrived overhead for rescue operations and continued to attack NVA positions. I remember Col. Bowman remarking that it was quite an event I had down there in Mo Duc.

I considered that an understatement.

Then he asked about the district chief, Lt. Col. Thanh. I related that I felt that Lt. Col. Thanh had been derelict in his duties to the extent that he failed to be the commander in charge of the defense of Mo Duc during the battle. Col. Bowman had many questions about Thanh's performance during the battle (and before it, too). I answered all his questions as forthrightly as I could.

We discussed the future of Mo Duc, Quang Ngai province, as a whole, our expected role going forward, and the ongoing Paris Peace Talks. He was a nice man and interesting to talk with. Eventually, he said he wanted me to brief his counterpart "Colonel Loi," the province chief of Quang Ngai province. Unfortunately, I am not sure I remember his name correctly. I think it was Loi, and I will use that name from this point forward.

BRIEFING TO THE ARVN COLONEL LOI, THE QUANG NGAI PROVINCE CHIEF: 1000 HOURS

The jeep drive from the Province Advisory Team 17 headquarters across Quang Ngai City to the Vietnamese province headquarters took about 20 to 25 minutes. They were expecting me and escorted me to the province chief's office upon my arrival. Col. Loi was a tall Eurasian man who stood about 6'4." He was a handsome officer, well built, and in addition to Vietnamese, he spoke French and English quite well. In fact, I suspected he may have been educated in the U.S. based on how well he spoke English. He was very polite and seemingly charismatic. We had a long and pleasant conversation that began shortly after 1030 hours.

Col. Loi was extremely interested in everything I said about the battle and asked meaningful questions for his further clarification and understanding. As I responded to his questions, he would smile or nod his head like he already knew the answer to his question. Throughout this informal one-on-one briefing, he would ask questions about cities or places in America. That sort of threw me off track. *Maybe he did not really care how things went in Mo Duc.* Yet, from his questions, I knew he was interested in how his Vietnamese soldiers performed, as well as how certain officers and non-commissioned officers (NCOs) performed. I held back on berating Lt. Col. Thanh, thinking that no good would come of laying it all out there. Loi did ask pointed questions, to which I provided clear and to-the-point answers while trying not to reveal my disdain for Thanh.

About 30 minutes into the briefing, Loi excused himself, went to his office door, and in almost a whisper, had a short conversation in French with someone. He closed the door and returned to continue our conversation. At this point, I really wanted to know more about his background, his story. It was likely that his father was French and his mother was Vietnamese. He was well-educated and exceptionally well-mannered. And he was interested in American cities. Our polite conversation continued until after 1230 hours and was enjoyable. I can still see him clearly in my mind's eye.

RETURNED TO MACV PROVINCE ADVISORY TEAM 17 HEADQUARTERS IN QUANG NGAI CITY

As I entered the headquarters, the Adjutant, Capt. Bliss, told me to report to Col. Bowman. He wanted to know how things went with my briefing to his counterpart. As far as I knew, everything went well, and Col. Loi seemed pleased. Col. Bowman revealed that he had talked with Col. Loi while I was enroute to the colonel's location. The discussion was primarily about Lt. Col. Thanh and that I had taken command of the defense of Mo Duc during the battle. I had a sinking feeling that was quickly eliminated when he told me more of his conversation.

After I left the Province Chief's office, he had called Col. Bowman. Apparently, these two men had a good working relationship. Much of the content of my briefing to Col. Bowman had been relayed to Col. Loi while I was enroute to brief him. The Province Chief began an immediate investigation through his confidantes in Mo Duc before I even arrived to brief him. Loi had learned that Thanh had cooperated with the NVA to ostensibly let them conquer Mo Duc. From my perspective, it was clearly true that he did not take any action to oppose the NVA surrounding the district headquarters or anywhere else throughout the district. Apparently, Lt. Col. Thanh had worked with the Viet Minh communists in their struggle against the French. Was he still a Vietnamese communist?

When Col. Loi had excused himself from our conversation, he received this information about Lt. Col. Thanh and had ordered someone to bring Thanh from Mo Duc to Quang Ngai City via helicopter. Col. Bowman then told me that Thanh would be replaced in Mo Duc, and he may have already been executed. I was shocked. To this day, I am not sure how I feel about that.

Col. Bowman had sent one of his province advisors, Maj. Kehoe, to replace me in Mo Duc. I would be reassigned to MACV Advisory Team 17 at the province level instead of the district level. I politely objected to this suggestion and said I would return to my team in Mo Duc. Without further conversation, he ordered me to have some lunch and then go to bed. I ate, found an empty bunk, and slept for an hour or two until someone knocked on my door.

BRIEFING TO THE NAVY SHIP
1530 HOURS

The Navy had requested a briefing concerning their involvement in the battle for Mo Duc. They wanted the person they had talked with during the battle to brief them "underway."

Underway, I soon learned, meant they were in the South China Sea doing whatever destroyers or cruisers do. They were not hanging around waiting for me—I had to come to them wherever they were. Within 30 minutes of the radio call, the helicopter arrived to transport me to the ship.

That was not much time to prepare. I didn't even know what I needed to prepare for. I did not know where the ship was or how long I would be on board. I relished the opportunity to meet the sailors on the ship who played a major role in the successful defense of Mo Duc. In reality, there was nothing I could do to prepare, even if more information had been given to me. The only uniform I had was the one I was wearing. My other uniforms, along with most of my possessions, burned in the bunker fire on September 16. My only preparation was to take my map, which was always with me, and wear my .45 pistol. On patrols, I always carried an M79 grenade launcher. My Vietnamese loved that, and I was fairly accurate with it. The M79 did not accompany me to the ship.

I had spent a year with the 1st Air Cavalry in 1966-1967, and, on this current tour, I had already been on several air assaults with local troops. The majority of my flights were on Huey helicopters. When the Navy helicopter arrived in Quang Ngai City, it was a sight to see. That helicopter was much larger than the Huey and had several rotor blades, not just one like the Huey. And the winds from the rotor blades resembled a hurricane! Loose items on the ground were blown upward, and a mini dust storm ensued. I hopped on the chopper and watched the local Vietnamese seek cover as it rose straight up quite a distance before leaving the area.

Within minutes, we were over the South China Sea and turned north. I am guessing that we were only several hundred feet above the sea. It was fun and exciting and it turned my thoughts away from anything land-based for the moment. If it took an hour to find the destroyer, that would have been fine with me. But it only took about 20 minutes to locate this heretofore rather large (but now seemingly much smaller) ship out in the middle of all the water. It had looked much larger from my tower at Mo Duc. I was now more comfortable than I had been in a long time. I was surrounded by Americans, headed for an American ship, and no one was shooting at me.

During the battle, I did not know the names of the two ships that fired for me. The first ship fired the most projectiles and was there when we needed them the most. The second ship arrived later in the afternoon of the 17th after the first ship had departed the area. Only years later did I learn the name of the first ship. It was the USS Hanson that I mentioned in an earlier chapter.

I could only hope that we were now looking at and intending to land on the first ship.

As the helicopter began its slow approach to land (or "set down," as the crew chief said) on the stern of the destroyer, I learned what was meant by "rolling seas." I had no way of knowing how tall the waves were. The ship was going up and down with the waves. My sense of being comfortable vanished. There was no way landing on this ship was going to be a good thing. Apparently, my thoughts were being transmitted through my eyes. The crew chief sitting in the doorway was smiling... no, he was laughing.

"Hey sir, is this your first landing at sea?" he said over the intercom.

I will not write what I actually said, but the translation would be "yes." He explained how the pilot was in tune with the rise and fall of the ship, and, when close enough, would cut his engine power to set down near the top of the rise. It was a smooth "set down," and I was comfortable again. But this ship did not look like the one I saw from the tower in Mo Duc—it was considerably larger. I soon learned that it was a cruiser and had fired for me. Apparently, destroyers do not have a helipad.

Bummer!

I was greeted by the ship's executive officer (XO), who took me to see the captain. He was in charge of the ship, but he was referred to as captain, not commander. While talking with the captain and others who had gathered, a young sailor approached me, requesting that I follow him. I thought there were a few snickers, but I followed him anyway. He led me to an exceedingly small private space with bunks called officers' quarters, handed me a set of Navy work clothes, and showed me the shower. After my shower, I was to wear the Navy clothes while mine were being washed. He assured me my uniform would be returned as quickly as possible. These were the same clothes I wore on September 15 and put back on the morning of the battle. Those Navy guys just were not accustomed to being around "hard-working" infantry soldiers, I guess.

After my shower, I felt *sooo good*. Life began to get better.

What an environment those Navy guys had: an abundant supply of clean and clear water, three designated hot meals each day, on-order hamburgers/hot dogs/sandwiches 24 hours a day, movies, laundry facilities, good protection from the elements, white sheets, mattresses, and more. I wondered how long I could stretch out my visit on this ship.

After a warm shower, hot evening meal, and getting back into my Army fatigues, it was time to tell them what kind of targets they had engaged several days ago. My briefing to the ship was done on closed-circuit television. This briefing was heard by almost all of the crew. By the end of the briefing, they knew that my soldiers and I were so very grateful for their gunfire and assistance. And we were. After all, they had helped save our lives.

After the briefing, I toured their gunnery room. It looked like a typical field artillery fire direction center, only cleaner, brighter, and more organized. (This is not meant as a derogatory comment directed toward the Army.) With their rolling seas and periods of bad weather, every piece of equipment had a place for storage that would withstand violent motion without getting loose or broken. They called their officer-in-charge the gunnery officer. A fire mission was received and fired while I observed. *That* was exciting for me. After the Navy fire mission, I toured the 5"/38 gun locations. I was glad I was not in one of the turrets when they fired. That had to be louder than field artillery, and we had enough trouble with our hearing as artillerymen. Their gun crews were about the same number of cannoneers, as we call them. It was my impression that cross-training Navy gun crews with field artillery weapons or vice versa could be accomplished in a relatively short period of time.

The XO then took me to the bridge. It was interesting to see how they ran and commanded the ship. When I commented that everything was metal and not too comfortable to hang around for a long time, the captain said, "That's the idea."

20 SEPTEMBER 1972, WEDNESDAY

Those Navy guys get up early. Some kind of bell system sounded with shift changes around 0800 hours. If you were going on shift, you had to eat breakfast before then. That day, I was awakened at 0615. The cruiser had a mission to attack a missile site in North Vietnam near Haiphong Harbor, and I was invited to go along with them. *So exciting!* Instead of the NVA putting it on me, now I had a chance to take it to them. I liked these guys. I wanted to go. *I'm ready to join the Navy.* There was just one problem. If I went, it would be another day or two, maybe, before they returned to this area. By then, Maj. Kehoe would have my Mo Duc team with no chance of me getting it back, I thought. I had to decline their invitation.

That large helicopter arrived just before 0800 hours. I watched it set down on the cruiser in amazement. Enroute back, the crew chief said they had instructions to take me to Quang Ngai City, but I talked with the pilot and convinced him that was an error. My duty station was Mo Duc. He agreed to take me home to Mo Duc. Had I not done that, I would have probably lost my team. Still might.

RETURN TO MO DUC

Upon arrival, I thanked Maj. Kehoe for looking after things for me and put him on the helicopter back to Quang Ngai City. He had not been told I was returning to Mo Duc or that he was leaving. He seemed perplexed.

Mo Duc was still trying to recover from the battle. There was so much to do, with debris everywhere and many repairs needed on the berm and perimeter. Our toilet and showers were yet to be repaired, and our water supply had been destroyed. Sammy was either in the village or in a makeshift local hospital somewhere recovering from being shot in both legs, and no one had seen either of his daughters since the battle. I hoped they were attending to their father somewhere. Much work was needed in many different areas in and throughout the district. Many of the homes were straw-thatched huts and had to be painstakingly rebuilt. Only the wealthier had stucco-type houses, and they, too, were small. Mo Duc district was a good example of a third-world nation. For example, electricity or running water or sewer systems did not exist. Their homes had open-end ovens. A fancy toilet was one in which you put your feet where indicated and squatted.

Well, I said fancy. They were *not* fancy.

I was pleasantly surprised to see that the 2nd ARVN Division had stationed an infantry battalion in and around the Mo Duc headquarters. The battalion commander, Lt. Col. Thao, was also appointed the new district chief. He was a career officer who enjoyed an enviable reputation. He also had a reputation as a night fighter, a great warrior, and an effective leader. This battalion was considered to be their special operations battalion.

Militarily, the NVA seemed to have mostly disappeared. The 2nd ARVN Division had conducted search operations throughout most of the populated areas of my district looking for the NVA, but they were gone. The villagers said they were not gone; they were just hiding in the mountains. The locals were busy trying to do their own brand of recovery. They were a hardworking, hardy group of people. Most were skinny, and some looked emaciated, yet the hard labor they performed day in and day out would have put most Americans to shame.

Otherwise, many repairs to fortifications, reorganization of units, acquisition of additional weapons, and recruitment of locals for the popular and regional forces were now required. I was asked to prepare an after-action report... I thought that was ridiculous. Everyone knew what had happened. Many helicopters had flown over and around Mo Duc since the battle. Of course, I wrote something. I just wish I had done a better job at that time and had included full names of many Americans and Vietnamese instead of just their job titles. Had I done a better job, writing this story would have been more complete and accurate.

Around noon, Sergeant First Class (SFC) Long and I took a jeep and quietly slipped back into Quang Ngai City to get a few pairs of fatigues and replace some of my military equipment that had been destroyed. It was to my advantage to keep a low profile there for a while.

21 SEPTEMBER 1972

On the 21st, Lt. Col. Thao and I spent most of the day planning operations for the next seven days. We seemed to be a good fit with each other from the outset of his tenure as the district chief. We agreed that several of our operations should be at night as the Vietnamese usually slept rather than maneuver or fight after dark.

22 SEPTEMBER 1972

In the afternoon, I received a radio message from Col. Bowman that the commander of all U.S. Forces in Vietnam, General Frederick C. Weyand, wanted me to brief him and his staff in Saigon. My presentation would be to all four-star commanders from each U.S. service at a briefing called a "Woo" or "Wu." I still have no idea what either of those words mean. I just knew it was probably something I did not want to do.

I did not have any fancy equipment or the time to prepare an impressive briefing similar to what they were probably used to receiving on a daily basis. They would have to be satisfied with hearing me ramble on about the battle without any supporting aids other than the battle map I always carried with me. Besides, these briefing gigs were getting old.

23 SEPTEMBER 1972, SATURDAY

A Huey helicopter arrived to transport me to Quang Ngai City airport—if you could call it that. From there, I was flown to Saigon on a C-7A Caribou aircraft. It was a different-looking plane with a high tail end and only two engines. On the trip to Saigon, the rear cargo hatch never closed completely, allowing me a great view of the areas over which we flew. It was a pleasant, uneventful flight. I was met by an American major with an Army sedan at Ben Hoa Air Base and taken to a hotel in downtown Saigon. He told me that I could not brief the four-stars while wearing my jungle fatigues. At first, he did not believe I did not have a Class B uniform. But I stuck to my story of only having fatigues, and even those were yet to have patches and identification sewn.

My escort said the briefing was scheduled for 0900 hours the next day. The uniform for the briefing would be Class B. That meant khaki shirt and pants with no necktie and black army street shoes. Again, I told him I only possessed three sets of fatigues and boots. Nothing else. I gave the major my clothes and shoe sizes, and he returned in an hour or so with some clothes. I tried them on. Now, I am an XL. He gave me an XXL shirt. The pants *did* fit but required a belt to hold them up. But he couldn't find one, so I used my fatigue belt. He then gave me size 13 shoes when I wear a size 12, and I did not get a hat.

He did not care, so I did not care.

I stayed in my room that night, trying to get my thoughts organized for the briefing in the morning while I watched the sights down below in the street. I saw numerous American soldiers dressed in their Class B uniforms on the street. The street had several bars and restaurants with Vietnamese enjoying their city. This was a much different scene here than up north in Quang Ngai province.

24 SEPTEMBER 1972, SUNDAY

My escort major took me to breakfast at 0700 and then to the briefing area. The briefing area was large. I would be on a stage. The audience would sit in cushioned theater-type seats with each row higher than the row in front of it. It was similar to many American movie theaters. *How surreal. Was I really in a war zone? Had I been fighting for my life against a determined enemy just five days earlier?* Talk about having to be adaptable.

I also wondered about my audience and who I would be briefing. My escort said I would be briefing the "Woo." I had no idea what the term meant then, and I still do not know some 50 years later. I was told that I was to direct my comments to the U.S. Army commander, General Frederick Weyand. The Navy, Air Force, and Marine Corps would also be present with their three or four-star generals. There also would be many colonels and below staff officers in attendance.

At 0900, all of the brass walked into the briefing room. My escort motioned for me to take the stage. As I did, someone using a microphone explained to the generals who I was and why I was there and about to brief them. Imagine this: a skinny major in an oversized shirt with a fatigue belt holding up my khaki pants and my oversized shoes clunking as I walked across the stage. I most likely had the appearance and emotional mentality of the World War II 1,000-yard-stare soldier.

As I began speaking, someone switched on numerous lights all directed at me and effectively limited my ability to see the people in the audience. I started talking and pointing to my battle map as if talking to myself until someone asked a question. The briefing was over in about 40 minutes. Gen. Weyand was complimentary to me several times. But I was not impressed with the questions asked of me. I sensed that the audience was simply too far removed from the battlefield to be able to understand what was important to know and to ask.

My presentation was recorded, and I was given a copy of the tape later in the day, shortly before departing for Quang Ngai City. That tape remained stored in an unopened box carried with my household goods from 1973 until 2012. When a combat veterans group asked me several times about what I did in Vietnam, I was unable to deflect them any longer. I played the tape at their meeting one evening.

That was the first time I had heard it. The quality of the recording was poor. Oftentimes, it was difficult to accurately understand my comments. When listening to it, I, too, could not understand certain parts of the presentation. Thinking it would be more understandable to have a written version, I sought a civilian company to transcribe the tape. The transcriber did the best she could, considering the condition of the tape.

The tape was transcribed by Leslie T. Stanley, a certified shorthand reporter employed by A. William Roberts, Jr., & Associates in Charleston, S.C. The briefing as transcribed follows:

MAJOR COLLIER: On 16 September, a large NVA unit attacked Mo Duc. They have been identified as the second NVA division. This unit attacked the entire district and had a priority objective of the district headquarters.

I was the District Senior Advisor present at the district compound at the time of the attack, and primarily, I'd like to impart some of the things that happened. To explain this, all of the things you see on the chart or the map are enemy positions with the exception of the square, which is the district headquarters, an area approximately 50 by 100 meters.

The three circles indicate the subsector attack of OP, to my left, a small PF OP at a place Americans are familiar with, known as LZ Dragon; occupied at the southern end of this (inaudible) all of this mountain area overlooking the district headquarters, a PF platoon, OP called Thiet Troung.

The district headquarters has three hamlets around it, heavily populated. One has a large refugee center. To the northwest, the refugee center was due west, between headquarters. And at the time, Kien Khuong, the southern part, a larger population in the hammocks. At [0500] on 16 September, this siege, what I call the siege of Mo Duc, began. This siege lasted from 0500 16 September until 0800 hours on 18 September.

The threat to the Mo Duc district headquarters at the present time has diminished, but the fighting still continues throughout Mo Duc, and the vast majority of the land area is still in the hands of the NVA. The attacks occurred on several areas between [which] we had two tubes of artillery, a company with four PF platoons and headquarters with 30.

We had a ten-man force on LZ Dragon. The rest of the platoon was in ambush positions on the left side and east side. And 10 men from another PF platoon, again, the rest of their platoon was on ambush in and around the area.

Another significant point is down in the southern village of Duc My, where we had our company with four platoons. All four of these locations were attacked about [0500] with heavy artillery and mortar rounds and at the same time, our location came under heavy mortar attack. The artillery [battery] fell within 30 minutes, and they fell back to the company positions. They lasted until about [2100], when we lost all contact with them. So there are seven survivors from the artillery, the company, the wounded, who made their way into my location, coming into enemy lines near sunset, the evening of 16 September.

They tell me they are the only survivors. One of them was the commander of the artillery, and he had destroyed one of his 105s when he grabbed the thermite grenade and firing pin off of his (inaudible), And he had it in his hand when he came through the gate.

The small PF platoons were losses of 20 to 30 men. The 190 company down at Duc My village evacuated their OP and moved into the village office area, which was a fortified area to an extent.

The enemy pursued this attack and quickly had the entire populated area up at Duc My. I think it is noteworthy to point out that we had some communications from this company that they followed the instructions to go to the OP. Later on in the day, they contacted us that they were there, and we told them to apply pressure to the units that were surrounding us.

The next day, the ARVNs came in on an LZ combat assault, they were north of our position, and the remnants of the RF190 company did provide LZ security. So that (inaudible), tells me right there that that company, even though they were small and badly hurt, kept in contact with their command headquarters, rather than just going our (inaudible).

At 5:30 in the morning, we took our first attack from the northeast, which was limited. I later learned that (inaudible) several observed our assault from the large enemy moving in, and I later learned that from what the people heard, we were (inaudible) this force was three or four hours late moving into the position, and that probably was a significant factor which cause the ground attack on the district headquarters at 5:30 to become thwarted and to become disabled.

We would not have been able to survive that initial attack if it had been executed as (inaudible).

Typhoon was in its final stages, there was heavy rain, cloud cover was up, the Navy was out to sea, the Air Force could not fly, we were overrun, and I had no support except for the 120 people in my compound.

They consisted of three PF platoons, some civilian office workers, a command structure of the subsector headquarters and the two Americans and the four Vietnamese that worked for the Americans.

Throughout the day, we continued to have heavy artillery and repeated limited ground attacks. At nine o'clock in the morning, I had seen many enemy to the north and northwest, west, and south, and thus we determined at that time we were completely encircled at the closest point, 20 meters and the furthest point, 100 meters.

This denotes dug-in enemy positions to my east, the hamlet of Dong Cat. The enemy did not attack from the east but had positions which helped present fire going off the entire siege period. In my northeast, we have what we identified as a full battalion.

From the west, a full battalion entered the refugee camp, and from the west (inaudible) and the battalion was in the central OP, and we had the platoon areas that had full battalion within the (Thiet Truong) hamlet.

There may have been more, I believe that these (inaudible) at least one point during the attack, there was (inaudible).

GENERAL WEYAND: I'm sorry to interrupt, but we had no choice—can you continue this thing and (inaudible) I want to say that I'm terribly proud of you. Great performance that you did here. I hope I will be back a little later. We have a meeting of the internal heads sometime around noontime, but I do want to talk about the concept of strategy for the period of time, particularly after 2 October, I think we are pretty well set.

Basically, I want to work on getting—like this land area Major Collier talks about back in our hands, and this is true countrywide. That means there's got to be a lot of tender loving care given to the evaluation these hamlet chiefs, the district chiefs too, and I think it's very commendable that this particular district chief would end up being—learning something from this (inaudible) being strengthened, so maybe he can do the job by himself the next –

The board, is to turn attention of ours and our Vietnamese friends to the situation in their province, as opposed to this case.

(Pause)

MAJOR COLLIER: A small miracle occurred in that the air was able to come up, and we got air power, the Navy moved in right off our shore, and we got Navy power. The territorial forces, they moved down from Tu Nghia, this was just north of us to the southern end of their district, the NVA (inaudible) in the area south of there.

These two territorial forces were fired at a range of 10,600 meters, just 100 meters short. They gave us outstanding support. The FACs (inaudible) overhead one time (inaudible) they identified 11 more and (inaudible), indicated mortar positions, and I really wanted to show you what might be called division artillery located to our west, all through this area.

This is an overview. I will let you move into a diagram [we] have of the center of the activity itself. You might be wondering (inaudible) right here, this is our sleeping headquarters, and what I thought to (inaudible) had a daytime TOC, an office, a kitchen, a little dining area, pantry, storage. The district chief maintained his quarters in the west part of our home.

At 1540 hours in the afternoon, a 122mm rocket on fuze delay came through and impacted, rather exploded, in the air inside our bunk. It was at this time I lost my NCO, my interpreter, dog, all radios, all weapons, the ammunition caught fire, and the place burned.

Within three or four hours later, I had taken 10 direct hits on this entire area. I thought it was time we evacuated. I also learned something: That one well-placed hit had, in effect, wiped me out. I decided to split the Vietnamese TOC.

We put half of our representatives from each of the sections here, and he and I (inaudible), and other representatives moved to an area over here. And we ended up in what was a base of a tower and also changed locations (inaudible) the base of a tower.

We had frequent ground assaults. At no time did we have less than about five mortar firing within an hour period. Sometimes we had (inaudible) accurate (inaudible) they were becoming better and better as time went on. By 1800 hours on Saturday, the first day, this portion of the perimeter defended by the national police field force, which contained our district TOC, our military dispensary had been completely overrun and was occupied by NVA.

The same holds true for the school, air, artillery and basically, in that area (inaudible) we were able to remedy this in part several hours later.

It was occupied by NVA two or three times. We never chased them out of here but hurt them badly. Primarily, our ground assaults came from the northwest and from the south. There were strong ground assaults, but the main one being the last, which began about 8 o'clock, 18 September.

About five o'clock, 18 September (inaudible) and terminated around 7:00, 7:30, 18 September. It was also during this period of time that we were being penetrated and (inaudible). We were strengthening this area. All the way down to the south, the very things they (inaudible) with everything they had.

Repeatedly, I told them that they were taking fire each time passed, but it continued. On (inaudible)

Landing at a point east of our location, 700 meters, 600 meters and exactly 300 meters from the battalion of NVA.

Another miracle occurred in that (inaudible) just south of me that our S-2 was up with UH1. The fighters were just arriving with 500-pound bombs, and these forces went into action immediately and the two aviators were extracted within minutes.

I think had not these things been immediately available, we would have lost the two aviators. Generally, that's it.

Sadly, these events continued Saturday night and Sunday, Sunday night, until about eight o'clock Monday morning. At that time, we were able to walk the perimeter. As I said earlier. ARVN regiment arrived on Sunday afternoon and made contact with us in the east on Sunday and Monday morning.

The NVA withdrew to the west and northwest, and this portion down to the south, so we had a buffer zone which exists to this day. So my observations and those things reported to me include the (inaudible). I went around counting bodies, and I counted 200.

(The S-3) report of 265. All were on or very near our perimeter. The people of the villages told me (inaudible) and hamlets told me that the NVA carried away all their wounded and many of their dead. The bombing that took place over at (inaudible) near the (inaudible) with extensive Naval gunfire, primarily with the mortar position.

I'm sure there was a larger death toll. It was reported that (inaudible) the VC, I think (inaudible) they said the NVA, but low morale VC were chained to their positions. (Inaudible) We did not receive (inaudible).

At a point (inaudible) it was pointed out to me, and the way they described the dead, appeared to be chained up. Had it on (inaudible) 50 meters. NVA soldiers who were well-dressed, well equipped, observed anything—some of them had 7.62mm chicom machine guns which could not have been out of the factory more than six months. I observed two of them.

They were beautiful pieces of equipment; they were new, well-oiled, and honestly had not been used before or very much before. They had ammunition in abundance. Each individual soldier's body had 14 days' supply of foodstuffs.

(inaudible) and some of them, they took out a package, and there were three capsules, red plastics and (inaudible) the wrapped capsule had white powder in it. I suspect narcotics, but only a lab analysis will confirm that.

Basically, that's pretty much what I had to say. Are there any questions?

SENIOR STAFF MEMBER: Were you able to use any gunships?

MAJOR COLLIER: Gun ships were not available to me, as far as I know, sir, and I don't know what I would have done.

SENIOR STAFF MEMBER: Gun ships were operating in the area; was this part of the overall attack? At the beginning, you couldn't get anything in there, but (inaudible) we did have gun ship support in the area. They were in the (inaudible) they were in the area anyway, there wouldn't have been (inaudible) been enough beacons to go around.

MAJOR COLLIER: I have (inaudible) I spent early Sunday morning...

SENIOR STAFF MEMBER: Are your people trained in using the beacons?

GENERAL WEYAND: We just requested (inaudible) and beacons.

SENIOR STAFF MEMBER: Seems like in the area where you were, you can probably expect use of beacons more than other districts. You need to have beacons and get people trained, no reason you couldn't have support all night long.

GENERAL WEYAND: We requested 11 additional beacons.

SENIOR STAFF MEMBER: They go in there in lousy weather conditions and just fire away.

GENERAL WEYAND: *Major Collier did an outstanding job, but also the fact (inaudible) I was very interested that he was in this situation of being shot down. I don't think he wanted to mention it here, but he told me he was putting out (inaudible). That's the same situation up in the northwest. First time we've ever lost a Loach because of being stuck in the mud. Got stuck in the mud and couldn't get out. (Inaudible)*

SENIOR STAFF MEMBER: Who's in there now? Are you going back, or do you have a replacement?

MAJOR COLLIER: There will be a replacement in there until I return.

—I, Leslie Toole Stanley, Certified Shorthand Reporter and Notary Public for the State of South Carolina at Large, do hereby certify that the foregoing transcript is a true, accurate, and complete record. I further certify that I am neither related to nor counsel for any party to the cause pending or interested in the events thereof. Witness my hand, I have hereunto affixed my official seal this 23rd day of August 2012, at Columbia, Richland County, South Carolina.

The date of the briefing shown on the tape was September 24, 1972. The location shows as U. S. Army Headquarters, Saigon, Vietnam. The briefing shows as conducted by Major William P. Collier, Jr., U. S. Army.

My escort took me back to the hotel to change clothes. He asked if I wanted to keep the uniform. I told him I did, as I had nothing to wear to travel in back to the U.S. I could not keep the shoes, but that was no problem as I would wear jungle boots bloused in my pants. And that was the exact uniform I wore to return to the US and to fly home to Oklahoma six months later.

I flew back to Quang Ngai City that afternoon in the Caribou. I enjoyed flying in a Caribou. The plane was met by Capt. Bliss, who had orders to bring me to Col. Bowman. I guessed my luck in avoiding him had run out. The colonel thought I had disobeyed him, but I thought I had not. I told him I was returning to Mo Duc, and he said nothing. I took that as his concurrence.

I reported to Col. Bowman, who motioned for me to sit down. He stared at me for several minutes. Finally, he asked me why I was still in Mo Duc. We had a nice discussion. He conceded to my point of view and the fact that the Mo Duc team was mine. He smiled and, in a whisper, said he would probably have done the same thing. He added, "Next time, let's be sure we both are on the same page."

I was not really sure where I stood with him until I received my officer efficiency report (OER) several months later. He gave me a maximum OER. I was happy and relieved at the same time.

27 SEPTEMBER 1972, WEDNESDAY
THE VILLAGE BANQUET

I noticed that SFC Long had some visitors from the village. After they departed, he told me that the villagers wanted us to come have lunch with them in an hour or two. I asked SFC Long if that was a good idea. We knew there were a number of local residents who were North Vietnamese communist sympathizers. He also knew of some who were Viet Cong but had never harmed their village neighbors. Could this be a trap or a planned ambush? He said he thought it was probably safe to go. Besides, it was close to where his family lived, and they had not indicated to him any recent concerns. I suggested that I would feel better if we took two soldiers with us, to which he replied that would really not be necessary. I had never received pushback from him before, so I dropped it.

An hour later, SFC Long said it was time to go. To me, it was still somewhat too soon to be wandering through a village that only days earlier had been under the control of the NVA. But I went. We penetrated the village further than I had ever been. Just as I was getting ready to tell Long we needed to go back, we walked into a sight I had never seen.

Between 20 and 30 Vietnamese were standing together in a small open area. SFC Long said they were the elders and other officials of the villages and hamlets that surrounded the Mo Duc district head-quarters. One of them started speaking. I could not keep up with what he was saying, so SFC Long had to interpret for me. He said they were there to thank me for not allowing ARVN artillery and American planes to shoot into their homes or into the refugee camp. They admitted they had been conquered by NVA. He said they could have survived anything that was to happen to them except the death of their family members. Some family members had been killed by the NVA, not by ARVN or Americans. SFC Long said they credited me with preventing the deaths of many of their family members. Their speech went on for a while. His words reverberated in my mind.

I silently thanked God for leading me to make the decision not to fire on those people on September 16. To this day, I fervently believe God put me there at that place and time to minimize the harm to those people.

When he finished speaking, the group separated. Behind them on the ground was some sort of ground cover with food on it. We sat down on the ground next to the food, which was also on the ground. I sat cross-legged also with some of the Vietnamese. Others sat on their hunches with their butt only a few inches from the ground. That was the rural way, which was normal for them. Chairs did not exist in most huts.

Now, to put this in perspective. Some vegetables were part of the spread with a few green leaves. Their greens are picked from certain trees and boiled in water. Some of the leaves were not boiled. Chicken was killed by wringing its neck, and with the neck still attached, the feathers were cut off with a knife. Then the remaining feathers were eliminated by burning, after which the chicken was boiled. Upon completion of the boiling process, the chicken meat was hand stripped and placed on a plate. The boiling process only cooked the top layer of meat. Once that layer was stripped, lower layers oozed blood, which did not seem to bother them. When all the meat had been stripped and heaped on the plate, the chicken head was cut from the skeleton and placed on top of the meat in an

upright position. This plate was put in front of the guest of honor…
me! I looked down at that chicken head and slightly colored red
meat. And the chicken head looked at me and winked at me.

Yes, it did!!!

I had eaten a lot of meals with the Vietnamese. To avoid stomach problems, Americans had to pick and choose very carefully what
to eat until they adjusted to the various foods in the Vietnamese
diet. This banquet was no different for me. As I gazed over the food
spread, I noticed something I had never seen before at Vietnamese
dinners: chocolate. And I *love* chocolate. I just knew I could go light
on eating other foods and really enjoy the chocolate at the end of
the meal. There were 10 to 15 pieces, and I kept my eye on them.
If the Vietnamese started eating the chocolate, I wanted to make
sure I got at least two pieces before they were all gone.

The French had taught the Vietnamese a lot about cooking and
eating. Thank goodness they taught them how wonderful chocolate
is! Someone reached in and picked up a piece. Now was my chance.
I grabbed my piece while deciding to eat it in a few bites instead of
all at once as I noticed that the Vietnamese man had done. I eagerly
bit off a piece. *What in the world is this?* When I bit this chocolate,
something ran down both sides of my cheeks. I looked at SFC Long,
and he broke out in laughter.

"Not chocolate?" I said as red, watery liquid dripped onto my
uniform.

He said, "Coagulated duck's blood."

It was a delicacy to the Vietnamese and only available for special
occasions, and you eat the whole piece at a time. You can only imagine how disappointed I was not to have chocolate. I did, however,
appreciate the banquet. It was an experience I will never forget.

As we were walking back to the district headquarters, SFC Long
told me that a healthy bounty had been placed for my capture. He said
that the elders wanted me to know that no harm would ever come to
me inside Mo Duc district. At first, I took that statement with a grain
of salt, thinking they could not assure me of that level of protection.

Later as I thought more about it, I realized that these poor farmers knew everything going on and knew almost everyone. SFC Long said that they knew the local VC. As long as the VC activities were outside of their village and far enough away, the VC and their families were allowed to live in peaceful coexistence. I wondered how many Americans who fought in Vietnam knew that. At that time, I decided that I was indeed safe from local harm inside the Mo Duc district.

SECOND WEEK OF OCTOBER 1972
CAPTAINS PERSONETT AND POLING VISIT MO DUC

To the best of my recall, I received a radio message during the second week of October that Captain Joseph A. Personett and Captain Richland L. Poling were enroute to Mo Duc for a visit. I was overjoyed. I knew them only as voices over the radio and as the two U.S. Air Force aviators who were mostly responsible, by virtue of their unimaginable courage and skill, for my survival and the prevention of the district of Mo Duc headquarters compound from annihilation during the period September 16-18, 1972. Now I would have the great opportunity to meet them personally.

Our meeting and time together over the next several hours were wonderful. They arrived indicating a strong desire to visit the OV-10's crash site and the location of the 105mm howitzer that was one of the first weapons they witnessed firing at the headquarters upon their initial arrival over Mo Duc on the evening of September 16. Once on the ground inside the headquarters compound, they were appalled by the damage and wanted to see everything.

They toured the Mo Duc compound with great interest. Of special interest was the original ARVN Tactical Operations Center (TOC) that had been overrun and also demolished by mortars; the relocated ARVN TOC in the base of the tower; my Team 17 TOC, which had little overhead protection and had lost its roof during the battle; and my team's bunker that had been burned by the 122mm rocket on fuze delay. To them, things appeared quite a bit different up close and personal than what they had seen from the air.

We left the compound to visit LZ Dragon, known by the Vietnamese as Nui Khoang. From this vantage point, I was able to point out the OV-10 and Loach crash sites.

After walking through the refugee center, both men wanted to get closer to the OV-10 crash site. Still in the rainy season, Mo Duc had experienced recent heavy downpours, which again caused widespread flooding. This eastward walk could only get us about halfway to the wreckage but we did get them into the hamlet *near* the wreckage.

While in the hamlet, I told them it had been occupied by a full NVA battalion during the battle and that the enemy had fired at both of them while they were descending in their parachutes. All subsequent hostile fire they had received, including that fire shooting down the Loach, had originated from this hamlet. And VC sympathizers were most likely still in the hamlet. I was hoping to elicit a response of some anxiety from them. But... Nothing. Nada. They were two cool-headed aviators. I did watch their eyes and could see they suddenly became more cautious.

Our time together that day was super. They knew I considered them my personal heroes. Even so, I could not convince them to remain overnight. Our water supply and toilet facilities were again functional. Most of the smoke and odor in the sleeping bunker had been eliminated. New—well, maybe used, but new to us—cots had been received. Perhaps the food was not so great at that time, but it was edible and nourishing. We had no air conditioning, though.

I have to believe that their amenities of good food, air conditioning, beds with mattresses, an officers' club, very few insects, and greater security in Da Nang were more appealing than the amenities I could offer. I don't blame them for not staying overnight.

It was a visit I hold as one of my best days in Vietnam. I appreciated their visit more than they probably realized.

Thank you both.

LZ Dragon after the Mo Duc battle, October 1972. Major Bill Collier is seen here discussing various aspects of the battle to include the location of Capt. Personett's OV-10 Bronco wreckage, Capt. Poling's Loach wreckage, and two parachutes. Photo provided by Col. Bill Collier.

U.S. Air Force Capt. Personett is seen here making his way toward the general area of the OV-10 Bronco crash site, October 1972. Photo by Col. Bill Collier.

U.S. Air Force Capt. Poling enroute to the general area of the OV-10 Bronco crash site, October 1972. Photo provided by Col. Bill Collier.

Major Bill Collier escorting Captains Personett and Poling through the Mo Duc refugee camp, October 1972. Photo provided by Col. Bill Collier.

Capt. Personett near the OV-10 crash site, October 1972. Photo provided by Col. Bill Collier.

CHAPTER THIRTEEN
FINAL DAYS IN MO DUC

I N THE WEEKS FOLLOWING THE BATTLE, I learned that the 2nd NVA Division, assisted by the 3rd NVA Division in southern Quang Ngai, had been tasked to seize certain critical objectives in Quang Ngai province. The 52nd Regiment of the 2nd NVA Division was given the mission to seize and hold the district headquarters town of Mo Duc. We also learned that the 2nd NVA Division incurred heavy losses at Kontum in April and May 1972 and was not at full strength when it arrived in Quang Ngai province in June 1972.

It did receive replacements but was still reported to be somewhere between half-strength to two-thirds strength by September 1972.

During the battle for Mo Duc, that division's strength was further reduced by limited ARVN operations, U.S. Navy gunfire, U.S. Air Force strafing, and the losses incurred during ground assaults against the district headquarters and throughout the district. The civilian and military leadership in the district of Mo Duc estimated the NVA killed in action totaled between 800 to 1,100, with many more wounded in action.

At the start of the battle on September 16, six members of District Advisor Team 17 were physically located in Mo Duc. Our medic, Staff Sgt. Bassinett, was in Quang Ngai City getting our mail and other supplies. In addition to Staff Sgt. Jackson and me, the two team interpreters and two bodyguards/maintenance personnel completed our team of six. Two days later, by September 18, 50 percent of this team had been killed in action, and a fourth member was seriously wounded. Only Sargeant First Class (SFC) Long, my Vietnamese interpreter, and I appeared to be unscathed—although we had minor injuries that went unreported.

Upon returning to Mo Duc district headquarters from briefing the generals in Saigon, many personnel changes had occurred. First, an Air Naval Gunfire Liaison (ANGLICO) team arrived unexpectedly to join my team. As I recall, that team was comprised of a Navy lieutenant junior grade, an enlisted sailor, and two enlisted Marines. I had never heard of such a team and had not requested them. The lieutenant said their mission was to provide and adjust naval gunfire and tactical air support when needed. I thought the two forward air controls (FACs) and I had done a pretty good job of performing those functions during the battle the previous week. This was just another example of the generals and their staff in Saigon not knowing what was really going on in the field. I did appreciate that they wanted to provide me with increased support, but the jury was still out concerning the need for it.

Second, Capt. Malikowski, intended to replace my captain who departed in August, and a non-commissioned officer (NCO) whose name I believe was Sgt. Stone, who was to replace Staff Sgt. Jackson, were also in Mo Duc upon my return. The Vietnamese interpreter and bodyguard/maintenance team positions were also quickly replaced by the Vietnamese. Mo Duc District Advisor Team 17 was at the full authorized personnel strength of eight again. Even so, it was not quite the same. And it never would be.

It seemed that the 2nd NVA Division had retreated into the western Central Highlands of Mo Duc district, with some elements even returning to eastern Kontum province. Lt. Col. Thao, the newly assigned district chief, was in hot pursuit. He was more interested in being a warrior than a district chief, and that was fine with me. While Thao chased after the NVA, Capt. Nguyen performed his normal operations officer duties and functioned as the temporary district chief. They made a great team.

Some NVA soldiers were left behind with the local Viet Cong (VC). I believe their purpose was to encourage the VC to keep up the fight, even if it meant no more than conducting sniper fire, infrequent mortar attacks, and making us more cautious when traveling the district roads.

The amount of information Capt. Nguyen received from the various village and hamlet officials each day was mind-boggling. Before the big battle, they provided him precious little information other than that which was required for the village and hamlet reporting system. Now, he received daily updates on VC and NVA locations and activities. I truly believed we had won the big battle for the hearts and minds of the local population, as well as successfully defended the district headquarters. Was this one of the ways they were to ensure that no harm would come to me inside the Mo Duc district?

The need for the ANGLICO team was not apparent. Living accommodations in Mo Duc were inadequate. They had to be uncomfortable. And with nothing to do for several weeks, they were recalled for reassignment elsewhere.

Lt. Col. Thao was not accustomed to working with Americans. He spoke "some" English and was amicable to me. On two occasions, I accompanied him for short visits to see his wife and two small children in Quang Ngai City. His wife did not speak a word of English. However, I was able to entertain his wife and children with my broken Vietnamese. One of the visits included lunch. After becoming Mo Duc's district chief, he moved his family from a location in another province to Quang Ngai. My relationship with Lt. Col. Thao was everything an advisor's relationship should be with the person he advised and more.

Lt. Col. Thao conducted many combat operations. In the beginning, he showed me his plans and asked for my opinion, which delighted me. But he would not take me on his missions. After several weeks, I took SFC Long with me to inquire why I was being left behind. A number of his operations were overnight. A few were two- to three-day operations, which I later learned may have been outside of Mo Duc district and Quang Ngai. But the reason he did not initially take me was not one I expected. He had been told to ensure my safety and not to take me on operations where I might be killed. I let him know that the choice to go or not go was mine. After that conversation, I participated in most operations.

About one-third of his operations were air assaults. Several times we drove south into Duc Pho district to load onto ARVN helicopters. I'll admit, some of the ARVN aviators' tactics scared me more than the NVA.

My last air assault was memorable. Shortly after extraction in the Central Highlands, we heard noises inside the helicopter that I thought sounded like "spuut, spuut, spuut." Several minutes later, the helicopter began an autorotation to the earth, landing *hard*. Upon arriving on the ground, the skids were bent some. This was my first experience with the helicopter maneuver known as "autorotation." The realization that we had just been "shot down" and survived suddenly dawned on me as I looked at the other passengers. Two of them seemed excited. To my amazement, the others were very quiet, as if this was a common occurrence. In any case, everyone made a rapid exit, and rescue helicopters arrived about 30 minutes later. I believed we were in a relatively safe area at that time.

I was not mentally prepared to lose any more Team Number 17 members. I did not want to know much about their personal lives, so, consequently, I did not include them on most operations. There wasn't much for them to do with local security after the battle or with the Vietnamese administrative infrastructure. I was sure they were bored and probably wondered where I disappeared to every couple of days. Most everyone was overly cautious waiting to see what the ongoing peace talks in Paris would produce.

Near the end of November, a Navy ship called me on my tactical radio fire frequency. We had not requested naval gunfire in a month. It was nice to know the Navy was still hanging around to support me if needed. The caller identified himself in the clear as the captain. He said the annual Army-Navy college football game would be played in a couple of days and asked if I would like to bet on the game. My world was limited to Mo Duc district. I had no idea what was happening halfway around the world in the U.S. But, of course, I accepted his bet. My recall was one that Navy usually won more of those rivalry games than the Army. What could I possibly offer as a suitable wager?

Several days later, the Navy captain called. The Army had beat the Navy 23 to 15.

"What would you like to receive for winning the bet?" he asked.

Of course, I chose American food. "Eight steaks would be great if you could spare them," I replied.

He agreed and chuckled that we did not want much.

Later that afternoon, we were informed that a large heavy lift helicopter with our "winnings" in a sling underneath would arrive in several hours. I had expected to lose the bet and had prepared a suitable "winnings" drop-off for the Navy. When the helicopter made contact with me, I requested that he drop his sling on my small helipad and remain while we unloaded the sling and reloaded it with something to take back to the ship. The sling was an A-22 cargo net, or one very similar to those I had used in the 1st Cavalry Division in 1967.

Much to our surprise (and later dismay), our winnings were not eight steaks as I had requested. It was 100 pounds of frozen beef steaks! We were delighted. That is, until reality set in. There were four Americans who would love the steaks, and four Vietnamese who *may* enjoy the steaks. That remained to be seen.

We had a small refrigerator running off a small generator. How long before that many pounds of steaks would spoil? Not long! And what could we do with the remaining 75 to 80 pounds of beautiful steaks that would not fit in the small refrigerator? The answer was simple. We had a steak fry and distributed the steaks to the local Vietnamese around our headquarters.

We unloaded the A-22 cargo net and loaded it with our gifts for the Navy. I had wondered what the district chief was going to do with all the captured enemy weapons we had from the battle six weeks ago. He agreed with my request to send some to the Navy ship. We loaded captured weapons of all types and models onto that A-22 cargo net. As the helicopter took off and headed east towards the South China Sea, my team watched as a number of weapons fell from the overloaded sling into the rice paddies. In my mind's eye today, I can still picture that moment when the weapons were falling from the sling.

Approximately half an hour later, I received a radio transmission from a very animated Navy captain. He and his crew were incredibly excited to receive so many captured enemy weapons. After a while, his happy transmission was getting lengthy. I began considering how to terminate his conversation as he expressed his apparent happiness over and over again.

I soon found out that the Navy does not go through customs upon returning to the U.S. *No wonder they were so pleased.* They did not realize that we could, in fact, register and bring only one captured weapon home with us.

In early December 1972, Col. Bowman finally got wind of my helicopter being shot down. He requested my presence in his office, during which he, in no uncertain terms, told me to stop going on operations with Lt. Col. Thao outside of the district. He suggested that the need for any operations even *inside* the district was highly suspect now.

Everyone began to sense that peace, in some form, was imminent. The next two months were quite boring. Only a few poorly organized operations were conducted, and travel throughout the district was minimal. No one wanted to take a chance on being in harm's way. It was a weird and uncomfortable time to be in South Vietnam.

Photo taken eight months after the battle for Mo Duc and provided by Major Bill Collier.

CHAPTER FOURTEEN
FOUR-PARTY JOINT
MILITARY COMMISSION

27 JANUARY 1973

Unbelievably great news! We had just received information over our tactical radio that some sort of peace treaty had been signed in Paris, France.

"Stand by for further information." We could hardly believe our ears. Could this war actually be over soon? Did we dare believe that we may be going home? My American team members were all smiles and excited. They immediately began talking about going home incessantly. I, too, was overjoyed and began thinking and talking about going home.

Our Vietnamese team members were also all smiles and seemed to join in our jubilation. They were pleased the fighting would stop. Most of them were born during war years. Peace was not something they fully understood. However, it did not take them long to realize that if the war was over, the Americans would leave. They began to understand that leaving as soon as possible was what each of us desired. Once they understood our excitement was more about going home to the U.S. than the fact that the war was coming to an end, they seemed to fade into the background. You could almost feel the team loyalty unraveling.

In retrospect, our initial reaction to this good news was cruel regarding our Vietnamese team members. Today, as I look back on that day, I am sorry for the way our expressions of joy were received by our Vietnamese team members and our counterparts with whom we worked on a daily basis. It had to be a confusing and unpleasant time for them. But, even today, I doubt it would have been possible to have any other reaction.

Brief instructions were provided to the team in the early afternoon. These instructions directed me to pack all my personal belongings and report to Col. Bowman in Quang Ngai City before nightfall—a helicopter was being dispatched to transport me. The other team members were not given any instructions except to remain in Mo Duc until additional orders were received. No other information was provided. I attempted to quiz the province team adjutant, Capt. Bliss, but he professed not to know what was happening.

It sounded as if I would not be returning to Mo Duc. *That cannot be true. Why only me?* Being told to bring all my personal belongings sounded so final. Though, as one might imagine, I did not have much in the way of personal belongings. It took no more than 10 minutes to completely pack.

Soon enough, the helicopter arrived, and I departed. My rapid departure without explanation had to add to the confusion and unpleasantness of my team and Vietnamese counterparts. There was no time to say anything to Lt. Col. Thao, SFC Long, or anyone else. My departure was sudden and hurried.

I will always remember my American and Vietnamese team members watching me get on the helicopter. They seemed spellbound as the chopper blew dirt over them as it lifted off the helipad. What an unpleasant—no, *sad*—memory.

That day, I simply left Mo Duc. To this day, I am displeased with the way it unfolded. I could have easily departed the next day, thereby allowing me a final evening with my team. A strong bond of brotherhood exists among small-unit team members who have served together in combat. Regardless of our different nationalities, the Mo Duc team's bond was strong.

Upon my arrival in Quang Ngai City, the excitement level in the American community was even higher than it had been in Mo Duc. The province-level American community was substantially larger than its counterpart in the districts. Why was everyone so excited? The answer was simple: We were going home soon.

But when? Who was to leave first, second, or third? We wanted details; however, no one knew the time schedule for anything.

A briefing was scheduled for that evening, so I joined the gaiety, primarily for the expectation of a good meal that night.

The briefing was very informative. We were told that a document entitled "An Agreement on Ending the War and Restoring Peace in Vietnam" had been signed in Paris, France, by "four parties." The four parties were the Democratic Republic of North Vietnam (North Vietnam), the Republic of Vietnam (South Vietnam), the United States of America (USA), and the Republic of South Vietnam (RPG: Provisional Revolutionary Government), which represented South Vietnamese communists.

This document created the Four-Party Joint Military Commission. It would be comprised of a Central Joint Military Commission, 7 Regional Joint Military Commissions, and 26 teams based at various locations throughout South Vietnam. Each team contained 16 people.

Now I knew the reason for the paucity of information available earlier. The locations and team members of the 7 regional commissions and the 26 teams were being disseminated to American installations throughout South Vietnam.

At the briefing, I learned that I would not be going home any time soon. Instead, I had been assigned to Region 2 of the Four-Party Joint Military Commission, with duty on a team to be located on the former U.S. Marine Air Base at Chu Lai. Chu Lai is a seaport town and a district capital in Quang Nam Province, two provinces north of Quang Ngai province.

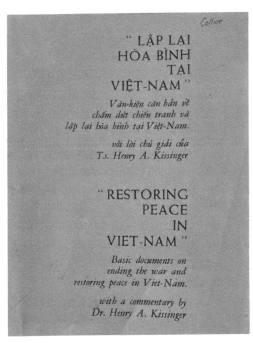

Collier

" LẬP LẠI
HÒA BÌNH
TẠI
VIỆT-NAM "

Văn-kiện căn bản về
chấm dứt chiến tranh và
lập lại hòa bình tại Việt-Nam.

với lời chú giải của
T.s. Henry A. Kissinger

" RESTORING
PEACE
IN
VIET-NAM "

Basic documents on
ending the war and
restoring peace in Viet-Nam.

with a commentary by
Dr. Henry A. Kissinger

This document was created and made public on January 24, 1973, and signed in Paris, France, by the representatives of the United States of America, the Republic of Vietnam, the Democratic Republic of Vietnam, and the Provisional Revolutionary Government of the Republic of Vietnam on January 27, 1973. A cease-fire went into effect in Vietnam at 0800 on Sunday, January 28, 1973.

But why me? The province advisor team had numerous majors. The reasons for my selection as a regional team member included my combat experience, my Vietnamese language capability, and the fact that I was the only American available who was familiar with all of Mo Duc and large geographical areas of several other districts in Quang Ngai province. The long and the short of it was that I could not talk my way out of serving on this team.

We were told that all hostilities would cease at 0800 hours on January 28, 1973. These 26 teams would be activated effective January 29, 1973, and they would be deactivated on March 29, 1973, as I understood it during the briefing.

Four members from U.S. Advisor Team 17 comprised the American contingent of the Chu Lai team. The team leader was my rater (boss), Lt. Col. Leland J. Holland, destined to be the senior American military officer (as a colonel) held hostage for 444 days in the U. S. Embassy in Tehran, Iran, by Iranian militants beginning in 1979.

Major Arthur Lovgren and another major whose name I cannot recall completed the four-man team.

For whatever reason, I was standing at the outside entrance of the Province Team 17 staff admin work area at 0800 hours the next day. It was a sunny, quiet morning until the NVA fired numerous 122mm rockets into the city. The barrage was completed in two minutes. The American compound was not a designated target. We decided that was the NVA's way of informing us that the hostilities were over for now.

In the afternoon, the team was transported to Chu Lai. We were provided nice sleeping quarters overlooking the South China Sea and a decent mess hall. The former Marine officers club was within a stone's throw of our assigned area. We spent almost every evening for those two months in that club. We were very much restricted as to where we could go on that installation, but one positive activity was a frequent swim in the South China Sea during the day whenever we so desired. It was great. The seawater was clean and clear, and I could see crabs on the sea bottom, some 10 to 15 feet deep.

Here is the rest of the story: An International Commission of Control and Supervision was also established by the Paris Peace document. It consisted of teams from Indonesia, Canada, Poland, and Hungary whose mission was to oversee the "agreement" and report violations. I cannot recall the number of members of each nationality on each team. The American team had four, as stated above. These teams were co-located with each of the 26 teams, according to my understanding.

These four groups or teams were co-located on the Chu Lai former Marine Air Base, in a relatively small area adjacent to each other. The Canadians were next to our small area on one side, and the team from Poland was on our other side. We all had an unobstructed view of the South China Sea. Close by us were the teams from Hungary, Indonesia, North Vietnam, and the Viet Cong. As large and sprawling as that air base was, all these teams seemed to be deliberately squeezed into a small area.

The teams from the four parties met each day at 1500 hours in a small one-story wooden building. The conference table inside accommodated approximately 12 officials. Other team members attending the meeting had to sit in chairs against the walls behind their team leader.

Lt. Col. Holland was the designated senior member of our team sitting at the conference table. He met this requirement each day except one. I was the senior of our team's three majors with date of rank. Lt. Col. Holland quickly learned the identity of the senior members of the attending teams. He and I would watch each day to see if each senior member entered the meeting building. If their senior member did not enter, then I had to attend in lieu of Lt. Col. Holland. I had that pleasure only once, thankfully. I sat against the wall several times. I believe the other majors did too. My memory is somewhat hazy concerning the details of these meetings. I had difficulty getting beyond the fact that representatives of four nations that had been engaged in combat only days earlier were now sitting around this table discussing the exchange of prisoners of war (POWs) and other matters. And they were doing so in a somewhat civil and friendly manner.

One of the missions of our team was to monitor the return of captured war prisoners and foreign civilians. In early March 1973, I was given the mission to return to the Mo Duc district to monitor the return of South Korean POWs. The day before departing for Mo Duc, I was handed a map showing where the exchange would take place. The ARVN would return captured NVA soldiers at the same time and location that the South Korean POWs were to be returned by North Vietnamese or Viet Cong soldiers. That location was in the southern part of Mo Duc near or at the border with Duc Pho, close to where the mountains began. It was also within the geographical boundary of Duc My village, which had been completely occupied during the battle for Mo Duc. Quite a large number of VC or their sympathizers remained in Duc My, I was told. Finally, I had something to be excited about. I was returning to Mo Duc, and to an area of which I was very familiar.

No weapons of any type were allowed during the exchange of POWs. That sounded like a good policy. Let us talk about this policy a bit more. I would be returning to a district where the locals credited me with playing a major role in defeating a numerically superior force. There was a price on my head. Duc My is the most communist-friendly village in Mo Duc district. And yet I was expected to just waltz into that area unarmed with no apparent protection.

Right!

The next day I was flown into Quang Ngai City and then traveled to Mo Duc by jeep. As luck would have it, Lt. Col. Thao and his battalion were in charge of transporting the NVA POWs to the exchange location. He and I had a joyous but brief reunion. I asked him if he would carry weapons to the exchange, to which he replied that it was not allowed. I think I may have cringed at his response. The Mo Duc district headquarters already looked different, with some of his ARVN soldiers occupying my former team house and sleeping quarters. The American Advisor Team 17 had long since departed Mo Duc and Vietnam.

Lt. Col. Thao walked me over to five two-and-a-half-ton trucks. Four of them were loaded with NVA POWs. He showed me his jeep and the fifth truck, which had his soldiers in it. Without saying a word, he pointed out a small arsenal of weapons and ammunition cleverly concealed in both these vehicles. He just smiled. I then revealed my .45 I had concealed with extra ammo, and he smiled again.

We were a team again.

He gave the signal to depart, and the convoy traveled to the POW exchange site. There, the prisoner exchange went smoothly. The NVA officers frowned at me, and I frowned right back at them. Twenty-one South Korean POWs were exchanged. Four ARVN soldiers were also exchanged, which we did not know about ahead of time. Thao and his NVA counterpart exchanged departing salutes. I thought that was interesting. The NVA headed west back into the mountains, and our convoy traveled north on Highway 1. Near Mo Duc district headquarters, I said my goodbyes.

My American team members had long departed for the U.S. My Vietnamese team members were not in the district compound, and no one indicated that they knew where they might have been. I am still sad that I did not get to see them that day.

On March 29, helicopters flew us to Da Nang. As far as I know, Maj. Lovgren, a Team 17 province advisor, and I may have been the last Americans to leave the Chu Lai Air Base. Most likely so.

Things were well-planned and happening fast now. In Da Nang, we met numerous other four-party Joint Military Commission team members at a site near or next to our embassy. All of us, including some embassy personnel, were loaded onto two buses. They resembled American school buses but were painted Navy gray and had thick wire covering all windows. Each bus had an armed ARVN soldier in the front seat.

Before boarding the buses, we were briefed that the security situation in Da Nang had changed for the worst during the past two months. We were advised to stay away from the bus windows. According to the embassy briefer, no one should have had any weapons in their possession. I guess the briefer did not realize that most of us were taking an approved captured enemy weapon home allegedly without ammunition for them. We did have to give up the ammo in Saigon. An armed military motor escort accompanied the buses to the Da Nang airport.

As the buses traveled through Da Nang enroute to the airport, I saw areas of Da Nang showing obvious evidence of recent fires and firefights. Da Nang had largely survived serious damage all these years of the war. If the agreement to end the war became effective two months ago, why had the fighting continued and entered the city of Da Nang? This war was not over. The "agreement" was just a way to get American troops out of South Vietnam. By this time, all passengers were feeling considerable tension during the bus ride. After a terse briefing making us aware of potential harm, with armed soldiers on each bus, a military motor escort through the city, seeing evidence of strife in a heretofore peaceful city, and being personally unarmed (or so they thought), we were somewhat concerned during the bus ride. But the buses arrived safely at the airport, and without incident.

Two U.S. Air Force C-141 Starlifter aircraft landed within minutes of our arrival at the airport. The buses went straight to the aircraft. We exited the buses and immediately boarded the airplanes. Within 30 minutes, we were airborne and flown to Saigon. I recall landing in Saigon, being taken to an area some were calling Camp Alpha, and being mystified by what was happening there. We were there to be out-processed. And our out-processing was accomplished in an amazingly short period of time, after which we were quickly transported back to the airfield. It seemed that operations at Camp Alpha had been scaled back to a "bare bones" capability within the last couple of days. The local Vietnamese were stripping the buildings, taking almost everything. We could use the latrines, and that was about all. Sleeping quarters were in a state of demolishment. However, the fact that Camp Alpha was being so rapidly dismantled no longer mattered.

We were on the ground in Saigon for only a few hours. It was still daylight when we departed Saigon on Boeing 707 aircraft enroute to the U.S. As we lifted off the airstrip and began our climb, not a word was spoken by anyone. I'm not sure we were even breathing. Eventually, the airplane captain announced over the intercom, "We are now out of Vietnam airspace." The yells and hollering that followed his announcement were almost ear-piercing, and it was *wonderful.*

We were really going home.

To the best of my knowledge, probably fewer than 150 U.S. military personnel participated as members of the regional Four-Party Joint Military Commission teams in South Vietnam. The certificate and the wall plaque shown below, as well as the "Restoring Peace in Vietnam" document, are most likely now prized historical items.

Each member of the United States delegation received their personal *Certification of Appreciation.*

A personal wall plaque, like the one shown above for Maj. Bill Collier, was made by the South Vietnamese for each of the four U.S. Army officer participants in Region II Team 4, March 1973.

CHAPTER FIFTEEN
GOD ON THE BATTLEFIELD

A
S THE CHAPTERS IN THIS BOOK were written, the need for this chapter evolved. I knew in my heart that God had to be present during the Battle for Mo Duc, that several events occurred that only He could have orchestrated, that the timing of the events was perfect, and that I could not imagine how each event happened as a matter of normalcy.

During the Battle for Mo Duc, I was aware that just when no outcome seemed available for me other than defeat and possibly death, relief in one form or another appeared. There were way too many good reasons for me to believe God was involved and that He was the one calling the shots when He saw the need.

As stated in an earlier chapter, I had asked God for help. I had put my life in His hands and surrendered to His Will through prayer early on September 16, 1972. I credited God with coming to my aid on several occurrences. Looking back to the battle, it is obvious that God was there. I am sure I realized the occurrences when God was present and exercised His Will. In fact, without my faith, I would be unable to explain these occurrences throughout the battle. Without God's intervention in 1972, I would not be around to "write and tell my story about the battle" in this year 2022.

As the events in the earlier chapters of this book continued coming to life, I also began to realize that so many occurrences in my military life had to be more than just coincidences. Life does not work that way unless you are fortunate enough to have exceptional advice and assistance from incredibly wise mentors along the way. It was not clear to me that I had been the beneficiary of such advice and assistance for many years. Someone was definitely looking out for me.

How fortunate that I was assigned to the Army's Field Artillery Army Training Center (ATC) upon my completion of the Field Artillery Officers Basic Course. In the ATC, it was rare to find a regular Army officer below the rank of lieutenant colonel. To the best of my recall, all the lieutenants, captains, and majors I met in my two-and-a-half years in the ATC were Reserve officers. They had attained the prerequisite level of education required for commissioning and had successfully passed the required physical, health, and training requirements in order to become officers. Initially, their goal was to serve their country by being prepared for combat if it came to that. After serving their active-duty service obligation, their intentions were to return to civilian life.

I was one of them. That was my intention.

Lieutenants entering active duty as regular officers usually did so with the intention of making the Army a 20 to 30-year career. Consequently, these officers followed a different path for their first 6 to 12 months on active duty. That usually entailed specialized training such as airborne, Ranger, aviation, foreign language, and advanced degree programs. By the time they were available for assignment to a troop unit, they were already "senior" second lieutenants or not too far from eligibility for promotion to first lieutenant. Their specialized initial first year or so of active-duty training had reduced their opportunity for early-on troop unit experiences.

The artillery training soldiers received in the ATC was, without a doubt, top drawer. Yes, the lieutenants were green, and in reality, they were learning along with their soldiers for the first few months of their assignment to the ATC. The non-commissioned officer (NCO) corps were the cream of the crop from day one of their assignment to the ATC. Except for the lieutenants, the vast majority of permanent cadres were combat veterans. To be able to spend my first two-and-a-half years in the Army in the ATC was to ensure I became a competent artilleryman. I am so thankful for that wonderful training period I had in the ATC. I believe this was part of God's plan as He prepared me for combat command in Vietnam and the Battle for Mo Duc.

Duty with the 1st Cavalry Division Artillery in Korea, 1963-1964, served to expand my horizons and understanding of the requirements and life above the battery level. My horizons were expanded even further on many levels during my first tour in Vietnam, again with duty supporting the 1st Cavalry Division as a 105mm howitzer battery commander from 1966-1967. There were many difficult obstacles and challenges to be managed almost daily in one way or another.

As I began to write each chapter of this book, my process was to recall as many events and stories as I could. As I thought through these difficult events, there was no doubt whatsoever that I had help dealing with them. The need for this chapter continued to be on my mind and heart.

In 1969, the gradual withdrawal of American tactical divisions and separate combat units actually began. By March 1972, almost all U.S. combat units had been redeployed from Vietnam. Ground combat responsibilities had been entirely assumed by the Army of the Republic of Vietnam, or ARVN as we called them. These South Vietnamese ARVN forces were still supported by U.S. tactical air and Navy gunfire with the assistance of American advisors, of which I would eventually be one.

After suffering significant losses during their 1968 Tet Offensive, North Vietnam rebuilt their military forces. With the U.S. combat units gone, the NVA felt confident enough to attack South Vietnam with their combat division forces.

On March 30, 1972, the NVA initiated an offensive, which our news media called the Easter Offensive when the NVA crossed the border into South Vietnam's Quang Tri province. At that time, most people in the U.S. read and saw pictorial news coverage of the battle for Quang Tri City and the Imperial City of Hue in Thua Thien province. The NVA simultaneously moved eight other combat divisions down the Ho Chi Minh Trail to various locations in South Vietnam. The 2nd and 3rd NVA Divisions attacked the western provinces of Kontum and Pleiku. The 2nd NVA Division then deployed across and into the eastern Central Highlands. I was later told this division entered the western mountainous area of Quang Ngai province and the mountains of Mo Duc district in June 1972. I also arrived in Mo Duc district in mid-June 1972.

By August 1972, to the best of my recollection, the only American combat military in my geographical area of Vietnam were advisors to ARVN units, province and district advisors, Marines guarding embassies, tactical air support in Da Nang, and offshore Navy support. This minimal force structure was probably similarly true throughout South Vietnam.

The Battle for Mo Duc began September 16, 1972, with coordinated district-wide artillery and ground assaults by an NVA Regiment of the 2nd NVA Division. I believe their unit was the 52nd Regiment. Typhoon Flossie was passing through this part of Vietnam at that time. The NVA had the element of surprise and must have known that we could not counterattack using support from the air or sea due to the typhoon. We were surprised by their attack, but based on my discussions in the preceding chapters, we should not have been.

How can I describe instances that highlight my belief that God was watching and intervened on my behalf during the battle? I will briefly provide circumstances and events, all of which have been discussed previously.

To me, 50 or so NVA soldiers attempting to attack us around 0530 the morning of September 16 was simply stupidity on their part, I thought, and it gave me a false feeling that perhaps our position was not their primary objective. Later around 0800, when we observed hundreds of well-armed NVA soldiers moving into the tree line 100 meters southwest of us, and we learned that they were supposed to have been the main attacking force, I thought we were lucky that they were late.

I will always accept all the luck I can get. But maybe luck had nothing to do with their late arrival. God had clearly intervened.

The remainder of September 16 was filled with exciting activities such as several probing attacks and incoming sniper fire, especially while I was burning classified documents, a period of psychological warfare, infrequent mortar fire, a 122mm rocket killing my NCO and one interpreter, and bands of off-and-on rain. God was watching.

I needed some good news. I was not very likely to receive such news, though.

However, in the afternoon, Capt. Nguyen gave me some. The Government of Vietnam artillery was now positioned near or at the northern border of Mo Duc or southern border of Tu Nghia. Our position was near the artillery's maximum range. At least we had our first awareness of some external fire support and help. This news was also a morale booster. Once again, God intervened.

Not too long after learning that we now had limited artillery support, our western perimeter was breached. I requested low airbursts on our position with one round at a time "at my command." I was unsure if they had sufficient range to reach us and how much deflection dispersion would occur at that range. I did not want to do more harm than good by killing nearby civilians. With my interpreter talking with artillery, we successfully put two rounds on and near our location. The NVA quickly withdrew. Again, it was another stroke of luck that we had received artillery support just in time before the attack. The artillery unit was reasonably accurate considering the range from gun to target, and the ARVN battery commander was professional and willing to follow my requests.

God had planned this scenario.

My Vietnamese soldiers quickly realized that the artillery could reach us and consequently reach the refugee camp and hamlet. They clamored around Capt. Nguyen, insisting that the artillery shoot the NVA battalion (or multiple battalions) hiding in the refugee camp and hamlet.

I am so thankful that God touched my heart and mind, resulting in my refusal to fire into the refugee camp or any hamlet. The significant actions of village and hamlet chiefs taken as a result of my decision could not be imagined. It was a major turning point in the battle.

In the years since 1972, I have often wondered and thought that God put me in that battle to ensure that friendly artillery fire would not be directed into the refugee camp and village-populated areas around the district headquarters. The decision not to fire most likely saved hundreds, if not thousands, of innocent civilian lives.

Was it coincidence that the weather improved in terms of reduced intermittent rain? The clouds were miraculously lifted. Around 2200 hours, two USAF pilots flying in an OV-10 Bronco made radio contact with me. They were forward air controllers and offered their assistance. Their arrival was key to our survival on the ground. God intervened.

The nighttime cloud cover started lifting, allowing the FACs to be able to locate Mo Duc. Several hours after the FACS arrived, an offshore U.S. Navy destroyer arrived.

Throughout the rest of that night and until the FACs were shot down around 0800 the next morning, September 17, they requested and directed tactical air strikes on targets they could see and targets I provided them. They also adjusted Navy gunfire and coordinated a host of joint service weapons systems. All this successfully orchestrated complicated coordination and activity had to be overseen by a higher power. God was the One in charge.

In the early morning, the skies cleared. By dawn, it was a beautiful sunny day in South Vietnam. A third FAC arrived on station over Mo Duc around 0730 to initially take control of directing the tactical air missions, thereby allowing the two FACs to concentrate on helping me defend my position as the NVA launched their "do or die" assault.

When the two Air Force pilots were shot down, the third FAC was available to immediately initiate the coordination for the rescue of those two pilots and two U.S. Army aviators shortly thereafter. These were not coincidences. God intervened.

He was also present on the trip on September 19 as the APC convoy made its way from Mo Duc to the northern border with Tu Nghia district. The river crossing, hiding among the palm trees, and the planning and thought process of preparing to run the ambush were enormous instances of "testing the mettle" of all concerned. God was in charge.

The sequencing and times of the various events reflected a perfectly planned scenario.

I went from feeling completely desperate early on in the battle to complete jubilance when I realized we were going to successfully deny the NVA a victory. None of the above events occurred as a result of my direct influence on organizations outside of the district compound. I felt like a pawn playing out my role as best I could during the battle.

God was on the battlefield and clearly in control of the battle to the extent of His Will. There is no other explanation for the successful defense of Mo Duc.

The battle for Mo Duc had an enduring impact on my life from that time to the present. I have heard stories of those who had survived combat battles and afterward had serious concerns about why they survived while others did not. I pondered that thought for a while and came to the realization that Jesus Christ was not through with me yet. For what purpose still remains to be clarified.

Yet I believe He has blessed and guided me throughout these many years since 1972. He allowed me to complete a successful 30-year military career as well as a second shorter career in the criminal justice system. More importantly, He was in my heart and soul during the birth and growth of my children and 54-year marriage to a wonderful Christian woman. Throughout my life, His blessings continued by allowing me to provide some comfort to others, especially combat veterans, and by providing me with a loving family, good friends, and pleasing relationships with others.

God is omnipotent and has always been present on the battlefield of my life.

—WPC

Colonel William P. "Bill" Collier Jr., U.S. Army (Ret.) Personal Wall Plaque

Major says escape miracle

QUANG NGAI, Vietnam (AP) —"I should have been killed," says Maj. William P. Collier Jr. "I wasn't. It was a miracle, an absolute miracle."

The American ground combat role in Vietnam has officially ended, but Americans are still involved in combat situations. Collier, district senior advisor in Mo Duc, is one of them.

Collier, who is 34 and a native of Portsmouth, Va., is a tall man who might be taken for a teacher. He and U.S. Army Sgt. Carrol Jackson of Tacoma, Wash., were in Mo Duc with 120 government militiamen when the district headquarters was attacked by more than 1,000 North Vietnamese on Sept. 16. Jackson was killed on the first day of the fight.

"We had had indications something was amiss, and I was up early that day, about 4:30 a.m.," Collier recalls. "We were trying to figure out what was coming. We found out very soon.

"The entire district was hit shortly before dawn. Firebase Dragon, on a ridge 800 yards to the west, was overrun in 30 minutes. The district headquarters, a cluster of one- and two-story buildings in a compound the size of a football field, was hit at the same time.

"Nearly 500 mortar rounds came in the first few hours. They were all around us. My team house took 10 hits before I decided to abandon it and find somewhere else to conduct my business.

"There was typhoon weather and we had no tactical air support and no naval gunfire. All I could do was notify province headquarters at Quang Ngai, 13 miles to the north," he said.

"Our headquarters got its first ground attack at 5:30 a.m. They had good cover an took advantage of the treeline. They got to within 50 yards of us before we shot them down.

"They learned their lesson—that we were prepared to fight and were going to fight.

"Within a few hours it was obvious we were completely sur-rounded. We were taking a lot of rocket and mortar fire. We had 120 men against a reinforced North Vietnamese r e g i m e n t, probably more than 1,000 men. I would say the odds were slightly in their favor.

"Time began to be nothing. It was just daylight or dark. I can't tell you minute by minute what I did. You evaluate where assaults are being directed, reallocate ammunition, gather information on troop strength, direct fire."

He continued:

"It was during the second ground attack that S e r g e a n t Jackson, the intelligence adviser, got killed. I was outside the bunk-er 10 feet from the door when it was hit by a 122mm rocket. The blast knocked me against the wall.

"Jackson was killed outright, together with our Vietnamese interpreter and Sandy, the team dog.

"That second attack was about the heaviest. They just filled up the whole area. They came in crouching. Some of them were shouting. Hundreds of weapons were shooting and you couldn't make out what they were saying. Later we recovered Communist flags bearing the slogan, 'To sac-rifice for one's country, liberate Mo Duc.' I suppose they planned to raise them above Mo Duc.

"The enemy had to be deter-mined because he was taking a lot of casualties. The compound was surrounded by concertina wire, and when they got to the wire they lay pieces of wood over it and climbed over. But they left a lot of bodies draped over the wire."

As collier recalled that day, "there was a lot of close-range fighting—point-blank firing with rifles and pistols and hand-gren-ade fighting. We were getting ar-tillery support by that time and putting in air bursts right over our own positions. That was a tremendous help in repelling at-tacks.

"But by 6 p.m. Saturday the NVA had taken the western peri-meter of the compound. They took that perimeter several times and each time were driven out. I can't say how many times it changed hands in the next two days. The cloud cover lifted Sat-urday night and that was the best thing we could hope for. The Navy came back inshore and the Air Force back on station.

"The odds were 10 to 1, but at that point things looked consider-ably brighter. The NVA put in an-other attack Saturday night and again before dawn Sunday. They came at us and we shot at them and we called in artillery and air strikes, and each time they were repulsed.

"Fighting was going on 30 or 40 yards from me. I was running around the perimeter locating targets for the Navy, calling in air strikes and adjusting the ar-tillery. All the time mortar and small-arms fire poured into our position. I was in shelters that took direct hits and once shrap-nel ripped through my canteen cover."

All through that time there was no sleep and the only food was rice which the V i e t n a m e s e "cooked over little campfires when there was a lull." Collier said his bodyguard, "whose job was also to take care of the lights, went around climbing up utility poles replacing bulbs. He got an AK47 bullet in the leg. It was a ridiculous thing to do, but that was his responsibility, and, by golly, he was going to do his share of the work.

"Help arrived Sunday after-noon. Elements of the 2nd Divi-sion were flown in by helicopter 1,500 yards from Mo duc and Monday morning the NVA put in their last heavy attack. It was beaten off and they withdrew. The worst was over.

"Only then could we assess the

COLLIER

casualties. I counted 200 enemy bodies in and around our perime-ter and was told they had carried away as many again."

Collier's wife, patrician, and Center in 1960-63, served as a bat-tery commander in the Field Ar-tillery School Brigade in 1963-64, and was executive officer of the Field Artillery School Resident Instruction Department during 1967-70.

Collier is serving his second tour of duty in Vietnam. His first one-year tour was in 1966-67.

Major Collier and his wife met while he was assigned to Ft. Sill and she was a student at Okla-homa College of Liberal Arts, Chickasha. They were married Nov. 19, 1961, in Seiling.

Mrs. Collier resided in Lawton for eight years while her husband was assigned to Ft. Sill and served his first tour in Vietnam. After accompanying her husband on a two-year tour of duty in Ger-many, she and the children re-turned to Lawton in June when he departem for Vietnam.

two children reside in Lawton, Okla. Mrs. Collier, a native of Seiling, Okla., is a substitute t e a c h e r in the Lawton public schools. The couple's children at-tend Sullivan Village Elementary School. Tricia, 7, is in the 2nd grade and William P. III (Trey), 9, is a 4th grader.

Collier is the son of Mr. and Mrs. William P. Collier of the 100 block of Sandpiper Drive, Ports-mouth. He is a graduate of Wood-row Wilson High School and the University of Richmond.

Collier has been in the Army 12 years. He has served three tours of duty at Ft. Sill, Okla. He was assigned to the Artillery Training

Ledger-Star, Friday, October 13, 1972

AFTERWORD

THERE ARE MEN who are said to be great, though most of those "said to be great" are only penultimately exceptional. Then there are truly great men in the purest sense. Colonel William P. "Bill" Collier, Jr. is among the truly great. And not just because I say so. His greatness is objectively true and proven, though the sublimity of that greatness may never have been known were it not for a harrowing 54-hour period in mid-September 1972 wherein he led a tiny, besieged garrison in a desperate defense against waves of fanatically attacking enemy soldiers and accompanying guerillas. Thousands of them.

Col. Bill Collier, then a tall, thin, bespectacled 34-year-old U.S. Army artillery major, was quite literally the man at ground zero who led, carried, and saved the day—actually, two-and-a-half days—when all seemed hopelessly lost.

Even Bill, now in his mid-80s, concedes that he believed they were all going to die at Mo Duc. There was no way his tiny little 120-man outpost located in the Quang Ngai province of South Vietnam was going to survive, especially when the fighting became close and, in some quarters, devolved into a hand-to-hand slugfest.

But survive they did, beating back a force that outnumbered them 20 to 1. Why? How? Because of Bill, and his masterfully innate ability to compartmentalize his fear (which all men have, but not all are able to manage), his ability to constantly assess the devolving situation and the collapse of his perimeter in every direction, his outwardly confident command presence, his judgment, encouragement, compassion, courage, and his unassailable trust in God. In addition, Bill's tactical and technical expertise enabled him to call for and coordinate supporting fires while running from one point inside the outpost to the next, with pistol (sometimes other weapons) in hand.

The attacks continued in succession: mass wave assaults supported by mortar and machine gun fire (even a 105mm howitzer, which the NVA captured early in the fighting) with green and brown-clad NVA soldiers screaming their battle cries while bugles echoed from their command elements. Yes, it was an eerie panic-inducing hell on earth with seemingly no way out. Yet there was, and this story details it all.

When I first learned of Bill's story, I compared it to Texas' ill-fated last stand at the Alamo or the British Army's successful defense of Rorke's Drift during the Zulu wars. I even said so in an August 2013 piece I penned for *The Daily Caller*, "Major Collier's Immortals and Their Fight to the Death."

Little did I know that one of the U.S. Air Force OV-10 pilots flying forward air control missions over the Mo Duc battlespace also likened Mo Duc to the Alamo and the Drift, as did my close friend, Col. (Ret.) Steve Vitali, U.S. Marine Corps, who fought to have Bill awarded the Medal of Honor in 2012. Bill had received the Silver Star in 1972.

The comparisons are undeniable. In the annals of recorded military history, there are only a few standout "fight to the death" battles where the odds of the surrounded defenders or those caught in a complex ambush (where there was also a huge disparity in numbers) were bleak at best. Throughout history, many of those who found themselves surrounded by numerically superior forces were doomed like the aforementioned defenders of the Alamo.

I'm thinking also now of Leonidas at Thermopylae, Custer at Little Big Horn (though different in a tactical or maneuver sense), and the initial Sikh outpost in the Battle of Saragarhi.

Some commands had the hand of God on them, like the Brits at the Drift, who miraculously beat back wave after wave of numerically superior Zulu impis and survived as a unit. Other examples are my own Marines at Wake Island, or the airstrip at Guadalcanal, and elsewhere; of course, Hal Moore's isolated battalion in the Ia Drang Valley in 1965, and a year later the Australians at Long Tan.

The Battle for Mo Duc was every bit as desperate as any of those actions, and but for a young Major Bill Collier, who took over in the dearth of senior South Vietnamese leadership, the command would have most assuredly been doomed.

God was with Maj. Bill Collier in 1972. God is with retired Colonel Bill Collier in 2022. This highly readable, pulse-quickening tale of Divine hope in the midst of grim desperation is a testament to that fact.

Colonel (Ret.) W. Thomas Smith Jr.,
S.C. Military Department
U.S. Marine Corps – Infantry
February 5, 2022

ABOUT THE AUTHOR

WILLIAM P. COLLIER, JR., Colonel, U.S. Army (Ret.), served 30 years as an artillery officer. His assignments included tours in Germany and Korea, two combat tours in Vietnam, and various stateside assignments, including staff and command duties with the 1st Cavalry Division (Airmobile), the 1st Infantry Division (Big Red One), and the Army General Staff in the Pentagon. In addition to the Field Artillery Officers Basic and Advanced Courses, Colonel Collier is a graduate of the Armed Forces Staff College and the Army War College.

He received the Silver Star, the Legion of Merit, two Bronze Stars, four Meritorious Service Medals, the Air Medal, two Army Commendation Medals, the Vietnam Gallantry Cross with Gold Star, the Vietnam Armed Forces Honor Medal First Class, the Combat Infantryman Badge, the Army Staff Identification Badge, and numerous service medals and ribbons.

Following military retirement, he was employed in the South Carolina state government for 11 years and retired from the State

Transport Police, where he was the program manager. Colonel Collier received his B.A. degree from the University of Richmond in Virginia and his master's degree from Shippensburg University in Pennsylvania.